99 Lives

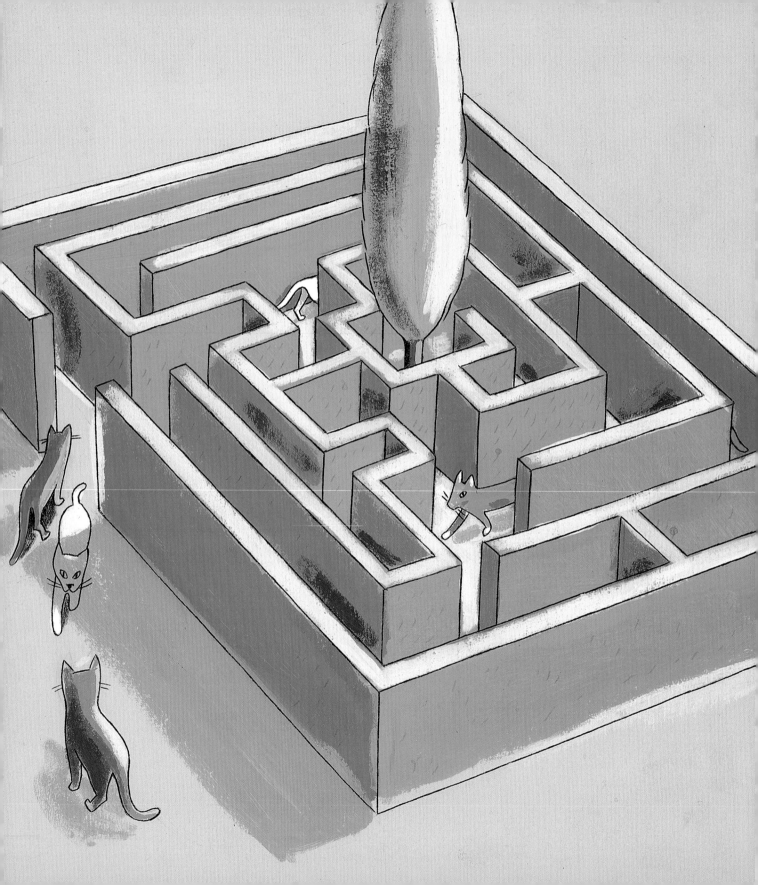

99 Lives

Cats in History,
Legend and Literature

Howard Loxton

CHRONICLE BOOKS
SAN FRANCISCO

99 Lives: Cats in History, Legend and Literature
Howard Loxton

First published in the United States in 1998
by Chronicle Books

A DBP Book
conceived, created and designed by
Duncan Baird Publishers
6th Floor, Castle House
75–76 Wells Street
London W1P 3RE

Editor: Ingrid Court-Jones
Designer: Gail Jones
Commissioned artwork: Toby Morison represented by Jacqui Figgis
Additional artwork: Annora Spence, Anne Wilson
Picture research: Julia Brown

Library of Congress Cataloging-in-Publication Data

Loxton, Howard, 1934—
Ninety-nine lives: cats in history, legend and literature / by Howard Loxton
p. cm.
Includes index.
ISBN 0-8118-2161-7
1. Cats—Anecdotes. 2. Cats—Pictorial works. I. Title.
SF445.5.L69 1998
636.8—dc21   98-16444
CIP

1 3 5 7 9 10 8 6 4 2

Typeset in Bembo and Linoscript
Color reproduction by Colourscan, Singapore
Printed by Imago, Singapore

Distribution in Canada by
Raincoast Books
8680 Cambie Street
Vancouver, B.C. V6P 6M9

Chronicle Books
85 Second Street
San Francisco, CA 94105

www.chroniclebooks.com

NOTE
The abbreviations CE and BCE are used throughout this book:
CE Common Era (the equivalent of AD)
BCE Before the Common Era (the equivalent of BC)

A cat's eye is the mirror

of the soul ...

Contents

Cats on Location — 78

Cats of Make-believe and Magic — 112

Introduction

Cats are increasingly the world's most popular pets: in the USA and Britain they exceed the number of pet dogs, so what is the secret of their appeal? In purely practical terms cats are less demanding than dogs. They tend to eat less; they can be toilet-trained; they don't have to be taken for walks; they rarely disturb us with noise; and they are relaxing creatures to have around — whether smooth and svelte or luxuriantly furred, their elegance appeals to our aesthetic sense. But these virtues might also be used to describe a household ornament. There is something much more important that makes us want to share our lives with cats — their varied characters and their very individual personalities.

Cats are among the more recent animals to be domesticated. Terracotta figures, discovered at Halicar in Turkey and showing women at play with cats, indicate that felines were domesticated some 7,000 years ago. And we know from tomb paintings that they were kept as household animals in ancient Egypt. However, both these examples date from long after the domestication of dogs.

Millennia of canine domestication, training, selective breeding and hunting have produced a huge variation in size, type and character of dogs. In comparison, the cat has remained little changed from its wild relations. Even the deliberate creations of late-twentieth-century breeders have made only very superficial differences to coat and conformation. The cat, again unlike the dog, does not live in packs in the wild — its instincts and independence remain largely unchanged despite its association with humanity. This instinctive edge may be the key to the cat's appeal, enticing us to own a "tiger on the hearth".

Yet the appeal of the cat's intrinsic wildness is only half the story. Hand-rearing a pet may extend its juvenile behaviour, the animal treating its keeper as a surrogate mother. The interaction between cat and owner, especially when the animal has been separated from its mother, involves a level of dependence on the human as provider and protector, but still the cat does not become a subservient member of a human pack. How the contract between cat and owner manifests itself will reflect the bonding that has taken place. It is certainly not one-sided, for humans, as well as cats, gain in many ways from the relationship.

Much of the pet cat's behaviour can be explained by bearing in mind its basic instincts and life patterns before domestication, but each cat is very much an individual and every cat lives in different domestic circumstances. It is the charm, fascination and, sometimes, downright cussedness of each cat's personality that makes the feline such a wonderful companion.

In this book you will find cats from around the world and throughout history who, between them, display the whole range of both instinctive and personal qualities that are to be found in the domestic cat. Cat owners may not immediately recognize their own cat among them but they will continually relate to aspects of behaviour that they will know well from their own experiences. Hidden among these pages are darlings and demons, mischievous moggies and pampered pedigrees, street-wise alley cats and posh pussies from royal palaces; there are real cats from history and imaginary felines from fiction.

Domestic cats share many similarities with their larger ancestors. In this detail from Benozzo Gozzoli's Journey of the Magi *(1453–1478), the cats are identified as leopards, but look more like what we know as cheetah. During the 15th century, members of nobility sometimes kept big cats as pets, just as we keep small cats today.*

Large gray numbers relating to 99 specific cats direct the reader to an extra nugget of information about that cat, listed in the *99 Cats' Log* at the back of the book.

Many of the cats mentioned have famous owners – well-known names from history, politics, or from the arts and sciences, but here the emphasis is on the felines. If you want to know more about their keepers you must look elsewhere. However, the fact that cats are kept by such a wide range of powerful and influential people is, in itself, a tribute to their wide appeal and the pleasure that they give to people from all walks of life.

It is perhaps not suprising that writers' cats like to sit with their owners at their desks, or that artists' cats enjoy playing with paint brushes, for the cats' participation can

be more than merely passive – it can be inspirational. Often, though, they are just showing their attachment to us by joining in whatever we are doing.

Sometimes cats will display their affection in stranger and more unexpected ways, as poet W.H. Auden found, "Cats can be funny, and have the oddest ways of showing they're glad to see you. Rumiface [his cat] always peed in our shoes." Nevertheless, we still seem to get the best of the deal. Or do we? If we sit and think about our own behaviour with our beloved cats, can we find instances of the pattern of our lives being dictated by the whims of our cats? As French essayist Jean Montaigne most succinctly put it, "Who knows but I make my cat more sport than she makes me?"

Personalities

Just as every owner has his or her own passions
and pet-hates, so every cat has its own preferences
and eccentricities. While we can generalize about
certain feline characteristics, such as the craziness of
darting from one place to another at certain times
of day (usually around midnight), and the apparently
reluctant, but secretly adored, air of companionship,
there is no doubt that each cat is unique – as different
from another as a piece of cheese from a mouse.

Cat Chat

Both cats and humans communicate through a mixture of sounds, actions, body language and scent signals. Humans are particularly aware of sounds because we have evolved a complex form of speech but cats, too, can make a wide range of vocal noises. These range from the steady purr made when a cat is content (or sometimes when it is hurt or sick), through the howls of courtship and mating, to spits and growls, chirrups and a whole range of meows. There is some inter-cat vocalization, with different types of sounds for talking to kittens or adults, but a cat uses its voice much more to converse with humans.

Kittens' demands for attention are easy to recognize. The white kitten raises its tail in a confident greeting in this painting by Fanny Moody (1861–1897).

Communication with humans often incorporates specific calls or patterns of behaviour that cats have been taught or have found effective. British novelist Kingsley Amis was convinced that his cat, Sarah Snow, was trying to speak English. Her attempts to communicate led him to write in a poem, "I was impressed to hear her say 'Hello,' Not like a person, true;/It might not sound quite right to you,/More of a simple squeak or squawk –/Still, that's what happens when cats talk." Sachiko, a sealpoint Siamese belonging to the author of this book, had a call sounding like "oweer", which everyone said was clearly an attempt to call his name, Howard. She used it in different tones to mean either "Hello, you're home – I'm upstairs," "Hello, I've just come in," or "Where are you? I want you!" – but she never used this sound with anyone else.

Adult cats, like these Three Cats by B.C. Norton, intercommunicate more through body language than vocal sounds. But a mother cat uses a mixture of greeting murmurs, chirruped orders and reassuring crooning with her kittens.

Sense and Sensitivity

Cats are in every way sensitive and sensual animals. They love lying by a warm fire or basking in the sun. They like being stroked, tickled and scratched, and some even enjoy having their coats vigorously brushed. They relish scents, often at strengths that we would find over-powering, and will sit drawing aromas into their open mouths to savour smells through a scent organ that humans lack. In their natural lives they rely upon careful decoding of sensory information for their safety, to hunt, and to locate mates.

Cats also have an amazing sense of balance and the ability to effectively land on their feet. For example, ginger-and-white Gros Minou survived a 200-foot (60-m) fall from a balcony in Outremont, Canada, although he did fracture his pelvis.

A cat's ability to hear is so well developed that most cats can pinpoint the source of a sound with almost exact precision. A reflecting layer at the back of the eye and a wide variation in the iris aperture enable cats to see in near-total darkness. Even gentle air movement and barometric changes can be picked up by pressure pads in their skin.

Some of the best demonstrations of feline sense-superiority are given when cats help less well-equipped humans, as shown by Ricki, a cat on an Italian cargo ship. The vessel had interrupted its own voyage to look for survivors from a small

This engraving of Sexuality personified as a woman shows a cat at her feet. The cat's acute senses led to its use in art as a symbol of decadence and indulgence.

aircraft that had plunged into the ocean. The search went on for hours but to no avail and, as darkness descended, hope of success dwindled among the sailors. But then suddenly, as if possessed, Ricki darted to the prow of the boat and began to meow loudly. As she ran to and fro to attract attention, the ship's searchlights were projected onto the water. A hundred yards away was a woman survivor – she owed her life to the astute senses of the ship's cat.

This painting by Louis Wain (1860–1939) conveys the cat's alert and gentle sensibility with exceptional empathy.

It is a well-known fact that a cat's heightened senses can make it aware of the imminence of earthquakes and volcanic eruptions long before humans feel the first tremors. One cat, Josie, who lived in the San Fernando Valley, California, gave the alarm well before the earth's movement could be detected by her owners. Similarly, in 1976, the day before the earthquake at Friuli, in Italy, all the cats in one village left their homes well in advance of the first shock waves and stayed away for two days before they came back. Scientist Helmut Tributsch, who made a special study of this earthquake, reported that in three instances mother cats carried their kittens outside and made beds for them in the vegetation.

Toto was an Italian cat living in the shadow of Mount Vesuvius. One day in 1944 he became extremely restless and that night he woke his keepers, the elderly couple Gianni and Irma. When they would not get out of bed, Toto persistently jumped on them, eventually scratching Gianni's face until he got up and chased him around the room Gianni was furious but Irma, a devout old lady,

In the Pinch of
Snuff *by John
James Chalon
(1778–1854),
the cat rubbing
against its mistress
leaves proprietary
scent marks.*

was convinced that there must be a reason for the cat's peculiar behaviour. She concluded that it was a heaven-sent warning and insisted that they quickly pack some clothes and leave. They had not long left the house when Mount Vesuvius erupted. As lava poured down from the crater, their home and village were engulfed and many people died. Their cat had saved their lives.

It is not only with natural phenomena that cats appear to be forewarned. During World War II there were many instances reported in Britain of cats who made their way to air-raid shelters or alerted their owners of bombing raids long before the sirens sounded the official warning. Sally, a black-and-white cat living near the much-bombed London docks, would leap up at a gas-mask hanging in the hall of her home and dash backward and forward between the mask and her keeper. Once outside she would scratch at the air-raid shelter door, then, when her keeper was safely ensconced inside, Sally would dash next door to warn their neighbours before herself resorting to safety. Another British cat, who earned the name Bomber, could tell the difference between the sound of British and German airplane engines – just as many humans could, but more effectively. Somehow he also knew that the German ones were dangerous and whenever he heard them he would head for the air-raid shelter, warning everyone of enemy approach. Although people would eventually respond to the sound of German aircraft engines themselves, Bomber's acute hearing meant that he heard and recognized the enemy airplanes first.

Cats are very aware of scents, sounds and small changes in temperature and air pressure. They will often sit at a window enjoying the "news" carried on the air, like A Cat in the Window of a Cottage *by Ralph Hedley (1851–1913).*

Cats and the Compass

Domestication in the cat is, in evolutionary terms, a comparatively recent development. While most live as pets with humans, many cats today also survive as feral animals, perhaps indirectly exploiting the presence of people as a source of food, but they are not strays. In fact, the cat who turns up on your doorstep may simply be prospecting for a better home – there is no reason to believe that it is lost, for cats are extremely good at finding their way back to base.

The Cat by Théophile Steinlen (1858–1923). Few cats are genuine strays – they have an excellent sense of direction and strong homing instincts.

Cats' homing instincts operate over considerable distances. There are plenty of examples of cats who, having been taken to a new home, decide to return to their old one. Among them was McCavity, a tabby whose owners moved him to Cumbernauld in Scotland. Three weeks later he was found at his former home in Cornwall, southwestern England, some 500 miles (800km) away. Murka took rather longer to cover 400 miles (640km) across Russia. She disappeared two days after being taken to live with her original keeper's mother, but it was a year before she turned up back at the daughter's house "dirty, hungry, pregnant and minus the tip of her tail."

Over short distances, it is likely that cats rely upon visual memory and recognizing smells, but over longer stretches, scientists have discovered that they may use a sensitivity to the earth's magnetic field. But even this amazing ability cannot explain how some cats have been able to track down their family's new home in an unknown place,

often a vast distance away from their old home. Such cases are often dismissed as simply similar-looking cats, but many examples are well authenticated.

Beau Chat disappeared in Lousiana while his keepers were away house-hunting in Texas. He was still missing when eventually they moved away, but five months later he turned up in Texas in the schoolyard where his owner was a teacher and her son was a pupil – a journey of 294 miles (473km) as the crow flies. Even more amazing, Sugar, a cream-coloured part-Persian, was re-homed when his family left California. Imagine their surprise when, 14 months later, he jumped through their window in Oklahoma, some 1,500 miles (2,400km) away.

Musical Cats

The normal night-time caterwauling of cats is not generally considered a musical experience, but nevertheless cats are known to have inspired several great musicians. When the Italian composer Domenico Scarlatti left the lid of his harpsichord raised one day, his cat Pulcinella walked up and down the keys, giving him, so the story goes, the idea for the sonata that is now popularly known as *The Cat's Fugue*.

Sometimes cats themselves took part in musical performances – a "Cats' Opera" was presented in London in 1758 featuring cats trained by a man called Bisset. Similarly, groups of cats have been exhibited at various times as feline choirs, or *miaulique* shows, as one Paris showman billed them. We can only speculate as to how they sounded.

The best-known musical cats are probably the pair of females heard singing in Rossini's *Duetto Buffo dei due Gatti* (Comic Duet for Two Cats), meowing their way up and down the scales. Maurice Ravel had many cats and in his opera *L'Enfant et les Sortilèges* (The Child and the Magic Spells), the Tom Cat and She Cat sing a bravura love duet in an authentic-sounding feline language, that had been devised by cat-loving French author Colette. *Paul Bunyan*, the American opera by Benjamin Britten and W.H. Auden, is another that features cats – these two are called Moppet and Poppet, and although gifted with human speech, they have a very feline way of singing it. Hans Werner Henze presents his cats anthropomorphically in his opera *The English Cat* so that they do not really sound like cats, and nor do Andrew Lloyd Webbers' in the well-known

Ferdinand van Kessel's strange painting of A Gathering of Cats *takes the idea of a* miaulique *show to its extreme. The cats in the painting seem pretty perturbed by the musical score with mouse notation!*

songs of his musical, *Cats*, although Gillian Lynne's choreography for the show reflects cat movements. Last, but not least, among this brief litany of cat music is the springing theme with which Prokofiev represents the cat in his delightful composition of *Peter and the Wolf*.

But what do cats themselves think of all this music? Some certainly have very personal musical tastes. Cody, a cat belonging to composer Henri Sauget was enraptured whenever he heard music by Ravel played on the piano. First he would roll on the floor, then leap into Sauget's lap to lick the pianist's fingers.

Companionable Cats

The independence of cats is a characteristic that appeals to numerous people. It also gives emphasis to the many occasions when cats offer or ask for attention and affection. The cynic may say that cats are only seeking their own advantage – warmth on a lap, human grooming or to reinforce a bond that ensures their food supply – but cats do offer much to humans. Stroking a cat is calming for the person as well as for the cat, and cats (and other pets) have proved beneficial in aiding convalescence as well as in combatting forms of depression and mental illness. For all of us, young and old, cats offer something that we all need – companionship. And they seem to take pleasure in our company, too.

A cat can share those moments of loneliness, insecurity or unhappiness that we hide from others, and give us reassuring, tactile comfort in return. Cats often react to grief or pain in humans with apparent understanding. Inca, a tabby-point Siamese, would always be on hand if his keeper was feeling low and on more than one occasion tried to lick tears away. Artist Henri Matisse loved the company of cats; and when ill health forced him to stay in bed he was joined there and comforted by his favourite black cat.

Cats also offer their friendship to strangers – we all know the pleasure of the unknown cat that comes up to greet us and exchange a word or two. The great Polish pianist and statesman Ignace Paderewski recounted how, when he made his concert debut in London at the St James's Theatre, he was overcome with nerves when he walked out onto

RIGHT *This pottery figure was made in Staffordshire, England, c.1850. Such pieces were popular mantelpiece decorations at the time, thus reflecting the increasing popularity of cats as domestic companions.*

the stage. As he settled himself at the piano, the theatre's resident cat came out to join him and leapt up into his lap. The audience was amused and delighted, the pianist able to relax, and puss stayed purring on his lap as he played the opening étude. Paderewski later commented that without that cat's presence, he could never have continued.

Cats are often very fussy in their choice of companionship. US author Robert Caras has described how a large black male cat, known to the household as Tom, would turn up only when his daughter Pamela was expected home from college for a weekend or the holidays. The odd thing was that Tom always

The cat in this painting Girl with Cat II, *by Franz Marc (1880–1916), seems happy and confident: it is lying in a highly vulnerable position, allowing the girl to tickle its tummy.*

appeared prior to Pamela's arrival. Her school was 200 miles (more than 320km) away, so how did he know that she was coming? Whatever the explanation, he always left the house when she went back to school.

Cats, like humans, can be jealous and possessive, begrudging any attention their keeper gives to others – but equally some humans can resent their cats being friendly to visitors. Often cats perversely make a bee-line for a guest who professes no great interest in, or even a profound dislike of, all felines. By contrast, some antisocial cats will go to the other extreme and disappear totally when there are visitors around, only to come out of their hiding-places when they are assured once more of the undivided attention of their owner.

"Stately, kindly, lordly friend,

Condescend

Here to sit by me, and turn

Glorious eyes that smile and burn,

Golden eyes, love's lustrous meed,

On the golden page I read."

from To a Cat
by Algernon Swinburne (19th century)

"Men ride many miles,
Cats tread many tiles,
Both hazard their necks in the fray;
Only Cats, when they fall
From a house or a wall,
Keep their feet, mount their tails,
and away!"

from AN APPEAL TO CATS IN THE BUSINESS OF LOVE
by Thomas Flatman (18th century)

Lazy Cats

In the wild, big cats exhibit tremendous bursts of energy when fleeing from danger or hunting for food, but otherwise they prefer to laze sleepily in the shade, conserving their energy for the next hunt. Similarly, the domesticated cousins of these powerful beasts spend enormous amounts of time snoozing in a warm spot. Kittens sleep for about half the day, and adult cats for even longer – on average as much as 16 out of 24 hours. But just as during a single period of sleep humans descend and ascend through varying levels of consciousness, so cats drift in and out of deep sleep, usually curling up in a ball when sleep is lightest and stretching out, unwakable, when immersed in dreams. Studies by the French psychologist Michel Jouvet have indicated that, during their dreams, even the most timid cats revert to predatory and aggressive behaviour, pouncing determinedly on imaginary prey, without showing any outward sign of this instinctive action.

Despite our insight into feline dreams, however, from a human perspective watching a sleeping cat has a wonderfully relaxing effect and is a sight almost too perfect to disturb. Such indulgence is illustrated in a story about the Irish poet W.B. Yeats who was about to leave the Abbey Theatre in Dublin when he found the theatre cat asleep on his coat. It is said that he was so loathe to disturb

This mother cat, exhausted from doing the washing, sleeps soundly while her kittens play at her feet, in a painting of c.1906 by Arthur Thiele. Cats are difficult to awaken from deep sleep and impervious to loud noises and disturbance – even familiar sounds that would normally attract their attention. Nevertheless, they always remain alert to strange and potentially dangerous signals.

This Japanese water-colour (c. 1850) is simply entitled Sleeping Cat. *Cats can rest in the most extraordinary places and positions. The ears in this painting may suggest that the dozing cat is still fully alert to danger.*

the sleeping animal that rather than wake it, he carefully cut away a piece of the coat's cloth so that the cat could continue its rest. Similarly, the philosopher and medical missionary Albert Schweitzer was totally captivated by his slunbering cat, Sizi, which had an unfortunate preference for sleeping on its owner's left arm. Instead of shooing the cat to another resting place while he worked, Albert allowed Sizi to doze on in happy oblivion, while he, though naturally left-handed, struggled on with his right hand.

Clever Cats

Many people think that cats cannot be taught tricks, but this is simply not true. In the early nineteeth century an Italian, Signor Capelli, had a troupe of cats who could beat drums, ring bells, grind rice, roast coffee, turn a spit, and draw water out of a well. Later that century, George Techow presented a circus act made up of cats who could walk tightropes, jump from stand to stand and through burning hoops, balance on upright bottles, as well as slalom around them, jump hurdles, stand on their forepaws and turn somersaults. Techow claimed that his best pupils were strays because the struggle for survival had developed their faculties. He maintained that he could not teach kittens, but took cats at one to three years old and then trained them for a further three years before they were ready to perform in front of an audience.

Scientific tests conducted at the Wesleyan University, Texas, have shown that cats have good problem-solving skills and are able to think their way out of difficult situations. They do better at this than dogs and are almost as clever, although slightly slower, than primates – and this ability makes them great in front of a camera. Movie and television cats respond to their trainers' instructions. They are not really acting of their own accord, but their ability to understand direction is testament itself to feline intelligence.

This pinprint, entitled Girl with Cat, *hangs in Wimpole Hall, Cambridgeshire, England. Clever puss has managed to jump onto the table to steal the milk, much to the young lady's horror!*

Most cats are better at learning for themselves than being taught tricks, for they observe things carefully. A nineteenth-century vicar described how four cats, who had seen the household dog rewarded for begging at table, were soon copying this behaviour so that they, too, could get tasty titbits.

After watching people open doors, cats often find a way to hold down a handle or push up a latch. But some cats never quite grasp why doors that can be pushed open from one side will not budge from the other, no matter how hard they try. One cat, called Tich, would always pound the door-knocker to be let in at the front door, even though the back door was always left open while Tich was out. Another cat, **Sampson**, discovered that when the postman

knocked, his owners would open the door. So, in order to be let in, he would rattle the door himself. The trouble was that he came home at all hours. However, when he found the letterbox and knocker tied up and silent despite his efforts, he learned to reschedule his excursions.

Cats soon realize that by doing certain things they can attract their keepers' attention and demand the service they require. It is amazing how they can manipulate humans by scratching at furniture, or in the case of one cat, jumping on the mantelpiece in frustration and knocking ornaments off one after another. A queen on heat who is kept inside can be particularly cunning. Sumac, a tabby-point Siamese, must have noticed that the upper two segments of a louvered window were rarely shut firmly. She clawed her way up on the edges of the lower sections and then pushed the top parts open enough to jump down

This cat in The Artist's Studio, *by Spanish painter José del Castillo (1737–1793), is being encouraged to perform his party piece – jumping through the loop made by the young man's arms.*

into the garden, free to follow her natural instincts and have a romantic rendezvous with the local toms.

Cats' cleverness, however, is not always put to selfish use. There have been numerous cases of cats who, on finding a house on fire, have rushed to alert family members instead of just escaping themselves. Boo Boo, of New Albany, Indiana, managed to awaken a sleeping keeper who had been sedated after being in an accident. Duke, in Kansas, woke the nine-year-old daughter of his family and then her elder sister. The girls rushed to wake their parents and Duke would not stop meowing until the whole family had escaped to safety. Cats have also saved owners from assault by flinging themselves upon attackers. Mouse, an otherwise aptly named timid and retiring cat, saved her owner Frances Martin by clinging to the assailant's face. Mi-Kitten, of Richmond, Virginia, found his keeper Walt lying on the floor after he had been mugged on his way home. This devoted cat stayed loyally by his owner's side and kept up a continual screeching until a neighbour came to help.

A sense of time, place and an unusual hobby combined in the behaviour of a cream-coloured cat called Willy, who had a set routine for Mondays. He always insisted on eating at 7.30pm, leaving immediately after he'd taken the last bite. By 7.45pm he would be at a traffic crossing waiting for the lights to change. Having safely negotiated the road, he then slipped through a hedge and took a short cut to reach a point where he could jump up onto a particular windowsill – and there he would sit, looking through the dining-room window of a residence for hospital nurses. And what did Willy find so fascinating about the nurses' dining-room on Monday nights? They played bingo. Perhaps he was not such a clever cat after all!

Curious Cats

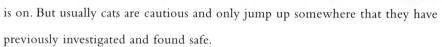

Are cats simply curious, or are they just vain, as Frank Paton (1856–1909) seems to imply in his painting Who's the Fairest of Them All?

As the saying goes, "curiosity killed the cat" – but is it true? Cats usually investigate the world with considerable care and their curiosity, if it can be called that, is an important tool that enables them to become aware of any potential dangers. They look, they smell, they reach out a tentative paw to test a temperature or to see if something moves. Their sensitivity to heat tells them not to let their paws make contact with something that will burn – although it does not seem to stop them from lying so close to a fire that their fur begins to scorch; nor can it warn them not to leap up onto a stove when the hotplate is on. But usually cats are cautious and only jump up somewhere that they have previously investigated and found safe.

There is always risk involved in investigating something that is potentially dangerous, although it is difficult for a cat to assess this when confronted with something beyond its experience. The English poet, William Cowper, described how he once found his kittens mesmerized by a hissing adder. Cowper rushed off to get a weapon with which to defend them, only to return to find their mother, her curiosity apparently aroused, patting the snake's head with her paw. He killed the snake, saving the cat from any dire consequences. There are many reports of snakes attacking and killing cats, but this mother cat had never seen one before and appears to have been unaware of the danger.

Curiosity has caused many a cat to make a misjudgment and has led countless felines into serious trouble. There are several stories of cats on board airplanes who, bored of being confined in a box or basket, decided to get out and investigate the cargo hold. Hamlet, for example, was flying from Toronto to London when he escaped and then either got trapped or panicked and went into hiding somewhere. He travelled many thousands of miles via Australia, the Far East and Jamaica before being found six weeks later. Another cat went missing on a flight from New York to Tel Aviv and similarly was found still on the airplane only after several weeks. Saucers of milk were put out for this cat in the hope of enticing it out of hiding – but Hamlet and another cat Felix, who disappeared for four weeks between Frankfurt and Los Angeles, are thought to have survived solely on condensation droplets in the hold. Other curious cats have been shut up in packing cases – one survived a sea journey of nearly six weeks from the USA to Egypt, even managing to produce four kittens on the way.

In contrast to Frank Paton's picture (shown far left) this cat, in Baron Balthus' 20th-century painting Cat with Mirror II, *seems curiously baffled by the vanity of its owner.*

Cats are often fascinated by modern appliances. A British cat called Victa was investigating a refrigerator when the door slammed shut, trapping her inside. She was thought to have frozen to death when discovered some hours later, but suddenly made a miraculous recovery. Harvey, a Persian, climbed into a washing machine and endured the first ten minutes of the wash cycle before he was discovered inside. Perhaps he was just looking for a comfortable place to nap, which is probably the reason that some cats climb into the warm spaces around car engines and find themselves involuntarily transported far from home.

There are a number of cats who are curiosities in themselves. Manx cats, either tailless or stumpy-tailed, and the bob-tailed cats of Japan have been around for centuries but are still remarkable when seen for the first time. In 1961 a kitten called Susan was born in Scotland with fold-down ears and

In Kittens Playing Chess, *c. 1860, by an unknown artist, this lively pair are interested in discovering what happens when the pieces fall over.*

became the ancestor of the Scottish Folds. The unusual ears are caused by a gene which also thickens the limbs and the tail. Another odd breed was cultivated in Pittsburgh, Pennsylvania, a hundred years ago. The cats were heavily-furred and dubbed "Eskimo" cats as they could withstand the temperatures in refrigerated stores. They were specially developed to control a type of rat which had also adapted to such cold conditions.

Curly-coated cats have turned up as mutations of other breeds a number of times in Germany, Italy, the USA and Russia, but it is two British cats from southwest England, that were the founders of the modern breeds, both known as Rex. One cat, called Kallibunker, was discovered in Cornwall in 1950, and the other, an unnamed stray of a different genetic type, lived in a tin mine in Devon in 1960. He fathered Kirlee who established the Devon Rex as a separate breed. Since then, other types with curly coats have been developed. A new American form with tight curls appeared in Oregon in 1986 from a kitten that was born bald, but gradually grew curly fur at about eight weeks old. Both this cat and its ancestors are now recognized under the breed name Dallas La Perm.

Even more curious perhaps, was the appearance in 1902 of two hairless cats Dick and Nellie in Alberquerque, New Mexico. The cats were said to be the last survivors of an ancient Aztec type, but unfortunately Dick was killed by a dog before he was old enough to breed, and as no other cat of similar appearance was ever seen, the breed died out with Nellie. Another hairless breed was founded in Toronto in 1966 when a black-and-white cat had a kitten with no fur. This kitten, called Prune, was the first of the new breed now known as the Sphinx.

This Ginger Cat *by Gertrude Halsband (1917–1981), looks very inquisitive yet tentative – the droopy tail shows it is feeling far from confident.*

Crazy Cats

Cats can be zany creatures, exhibiting some very peculiar mood swings. One moment they can be curled up apparently oblivious to the world, the next we find them careening around like things possessed, then, just as suddenly, they seem to run out of steam and return to their snooze. It is as though someone winds them up like clockwork toys and they have to rush about frantically using up energy until the mechanism runs down.

We can only speculate as to why cats behave in this way. Perhaps it is a cure for boredom or a ploy to ensure they get human attention. When the Siamese Coya heard her human friend Frances, who often wore a long coat, returning home, she would wait until she was inside the apartment, then dash down the length of the flat, and straight up the coat, to greet her.

This crazy-looking, psychedelic cat was painted by the British artist Louis Wain (1860–1939). Wain became so obsessed with cats that he went mad.

The chase is a natural part of predatory behaviour, learned in kitten play, which pets continue into adulthood. Such instinct often manifests itself in crazy, non-productive forms – what possible advantage can there be for cats to chase their own tails? – but its roots in natural behaviour are clearly evident. Inca, another Siamese, invented an entertaining game of retrieval. His favourite "catch" was a ball of crumpled paper which he would take up in his teeth and repeatedly bring back to be thrown again. Another of Inca's games was to push the bathroom door open, snatch the end of the toilet roll in his teeth, and then rush down the hall, unravelling it behind him as he went.

26

Predatory behaviour, such as carrying prey back to a secure spot to feast, is parallelled in domestic cats when they bring home mice or birds, but what triggers the hoarding reaction shown by crazy kleptomaniac cats? Inca used to steal underwear and hide it, while another cat, Sachiko, took socks from the drying rack and transported them to her food bowl. There she would alternately eat food and chew sock – pehaps her idea of dental hygiene. A London kitten called Ariel also has a bizarre habit – she steals her keeper's foil-wrapped chocolates and stashes them in the bathroom.

27

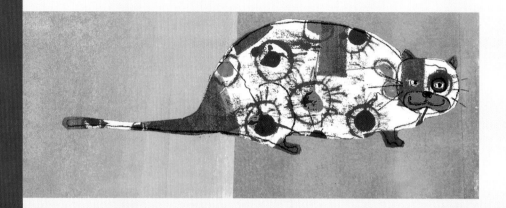

Boss Cats

Cats are extremely territorial and do not readily tolerate intruders, although they are always delighted to see their friends. In their own household they like a clear hierarchy to be established, and even if there are other animals around they expect to be the boss. A Siamese, Coya, was very protective toward her brother, Inca, but in return he had to do as he was told. When she learned how to open the refrigerator door, she let him raid it while she sat watching from above, supervising the whole operation. This meant that if they were discovered, it was he who got the blame while she was suddenly nowhere to be seen.

Some cats also expect to be top cat where humans are concerned. Cats like regular schedules and reliable service and can be very demanding if standards are allowed to slip, with meals late or litter trays left unchanged. It is amazing how quickly a cat can train a keeper! After his sister died, Inca helped to rear a new kitten and then got bossed around by her – but he knew how to stand up for himself with people. He liked to play a game every night before the household went to bed. On evenings when there were guests, he would greet the visitors, but quietly disappear to let the humans get on with their affairs until he decided they had stayed long enough. As his bedtime approached, Inca would appear and noisily indicate that he was missing his playtime and that all the visitors should now go home.

Some cats have a very strong sense of hierarchy – with themselves definitely at the top, as in The Chairman *by Louis Wain. If you do not want to end up as a lackey, make sure your cat knows who is in charge!*

When someone other than the owner temporarily takes over looking after a cat, puss sometimes has to lower his or her standards and accept a less indulgent level of care. Fa-shen, a tortoiseshell shorthair belonging to a television producer, normally has a diet of fresh fish with a side order of dry cat chow. However, when the producer is away on location and someone else has to feed her, she has been known to make do with canned cat food, if that is the only thing on offer. Of course, the moment that her keeper returns, she insists on resuming her proper menu.

Many keepers who commit the ultimate dereliction of duty in the eyes of their cat – going away and leaving someone else in charge – are met with complete indifference on their return, the offended cat simply refusing to speak to the miscreant who went off and abandoned the creature. If you have ever left a cat behind while you went on a trip, you have probably experienced how cats express their displeasure at being deserted. Some manage to maintain a sulky disdain for days before they admit that they are really very pleased to see you again.

An 18th-century print, after a drawing by Buffon, of The Angora Cat. *The illustration depicts the elegant longhair breed that became an aristocrat among domestic cats until new fashions swept through the World Cat Fancy.*

*"Like those great sphinxes lounging through
eternity in noble attitudes upon the desert sand,
they gaze in curiosity at nothing,
calm and wise."*

by Charles Baudelaire (19th century)

A Cat's Life

According to the French novelist Victor Hugo, "God made the cat to give humankind the pleasure of caressing the tiger." The cat's life has been modified by domestication, but its instincts remain those of a wild animal. From innocent kitten to affectionate companion, the cat can live happily beside a warm hearth, but always with a paw in the reality of its natural life as a hunter.

Cats in Love

ABOVE *The rooftop rendezvous of Édouard Manet's (1832–1883) lithograph for Champfleury's book* Les Chats *is immediately evocative of caterwauling alley cats.*

RIGHT *An early 20th-century cat in Wemyss Ware porcelain.*

Do cats fall in love? Most zoologists would consider this question a case of projecting human values onto feline mating behaviour. However, many owners of breeding toms and females can attest to displays of real affection between studs and their visiting queens. Cynics might interpret this behaviour as seductive rather than romantic, but in many cases cats do show an affection for others of their own species – as well as for humans – which seems to go beyond mere self-interest.

Cats whose matings are arranged by humans may appear monogamous, but if a female is separated from a male while she remains on heat, the urge to continue mating is strong and she will find another mate if possible. Where a queen is free to follow her natural instincts, she will probably accept many lovers. Male cats often have to fight for her favours, but however much a tom cat may swagger, it is the female who is in control. She may reject the victor and she will probably mate with a succession of males if she can.

The female cat informs males that she is in season through scent signals but she also uses a loud call to summon them. Some pets have learned to supress this call, at least indoors, to ensure that their keepers do not shut them in to prevent them from mating. Male caterwauling is not a mating call but part of the competition between the local toms. A male without rivals or a triumphant tom will court the female with little chirrups. If she accepts his advances, she will purr and roll submissively in front of him, but if he approaches too soon she may spit, growl, and lash out at him. The act of love is usually very brief and its end is painful for the female who gives a loud scream and may turn against her lover.

The cat's lustful reputation is well earned but it is the result of biological necessity for, unlike many other mammals, the female cat ovulates only in response to actual intercourse, so that multiple matings are necessary to ensure conception. This also means that kittens in the same litter can have different fathers and it partly accounts for the diversity of markings among siblings.

Queens and Kittens

Kittens are protected, fed and taught everything they need to know by their mothers. In the wild, when kittens are about a month old the mother cat feeds them from her kill and they may stay with her until they are mature. The arrival of a new litter demanding the mother's attention is often what finally forces them to fend for themselves. Domestic litters are usually weaned at two months and may be parted from their mother a month later – far from having to rely on their own resources, they usually turn to an indulgent human mother-figure.

ABOVE *The bond between a mother cat and her young is very strong, as shown in this painting by Jacques Lehmann (1881–1974). She is the centre of their world and her life revolves around their well-being.*

Motherhood is a demanding job, especially with a large family to rear. The average litter size is four kittens, but in 1970 Tarawood Antigone, a Burmese in Oxfordshire, England, produced an amazing litter of 19 kittens! However, the current record for a lifetime's offspring is held by Dusty of Bonham, Texas, who gave birth to her 420th kitten in 1952, when she was 18 years old!

If her kittens are endangered a mother will defend them fiercely, ignoring any risk to herself. During the heavy bombing of World War II, a cat in Portsmouth, England, found an ingenious way to rescue her kittens. The only way out of their home was through an open bedroom window but it was too high to jump from with kittens or to drop them to safety. Furthermore, there was no tree or drain pipe to climb down. There was, however, a telephone cable attached to the wall near the window. One at a time, she took her two kittens gently in her mouth, jumped from the ledge to the cable, and carried them along it, down a telegraph pole and into the garden shed. Whether or not she sensed the impending danger of the forthcoming air raid, or had a more specific premonition, she probably saved their lives, for, soon after they reached the shed, the blast from a bomb showered their home with debris and broken glass.

Another wartime cat, Faith, took refuge with her kitten in the church of St Augustine with St Faith, London, during an air raid, but her instincts for safety were thwarted when the church was hit by a bomb. Although Faith could have escaped alone, she stayed to protect her kitten while the debris collapsed around them. Happily, three days later, both cats were found alive.

Anyone who has watched a kitten playing will know that the cat's reputation for curiosity is well-founded. Kittens love to explore intriguing places, such as this basket, in a painting (c.1895) by Charles van den Eycken.

Cats and their Keepers

Whereas in the past people kept cats mainly as mousers, today we take them into our homes and rear them as pets from kittenhood. But "the trouble with kittens," as the saying goes, "is that they grow up into cats." It is easy to be captivated by a helpless baby animal but keeping a pet cat for the duration of its lifetime is a commitment not to be undertaken lightly. If, however, it is approached with the right degree of seriousness, it can be an endlessly rewarding experience for both cat and keeper.

Sadly, some cats are over-indulged by well-meaning owners: a cat needs stimulus and exercise, not overfeeding. (Himmy, a tabby in Queensland, Australia, who died in 1986, had the dubious distinction of being the heaviest recorded cat, weighing in at almost 47 pounds or 21.3kg.) In balanced partnerships the cat will be assured of a secure and healthy life, while the keeper gains an infinitely fascinating feline friend and companion, and a firm bond is established between them.

Cats are cunning creatures and it is often suggested that they exploit their keepers. Perhaps they do, but their humans are happy to allow themselves be exploited and actually get much in return. Some people have gone to extraordinary lengths to show appreciation for their pets. Katharine Tofts, an English opera singer, left bequests to 20 cats when she

ABOVE *Cats tend to be quite tolerant and will put up with considerable handling, as shown in* Young Girl with Cat *by Théophile Steinlen (1859–1923).*

LEFT *This kitten accompanies her keeper on a walk in* Portrait of a Woman *by Henri Rousseau (1844–1910).*

died in 1709, and there are plenty of examples of people who have bequeathed their fortunes to their cats. In California, in the 1960s, William Greer left $415,000 to his beloved Hellcat and Brownie, while, in 1978, another Californian cat named Charlie Chan probably became one of the richest felines in the world when he personally inherited an estate worth $250,000. At other times, the tables have been turned and the cats have helped to make their keepers rich — for example, by becoming stars of television commercials — but none so far has actually bequeathed everything to a human!

Writers' Cats

There are few relationships more mutually satisfying than those between writers and their feline companions, for on the surface only limited demands are made on either side. As the British writers Aldous Huxley and Muriel Spark both observed, a cat is perhaps ideally suited to a writer's solitary existence and, in turn, an author absorbed in his or her work makes a suitably self-contained companion for a cat. It is often felt that the presence of a cat on the desk or on the lap can help to induce a kind of meditative concentration that stimulates the powers of the imagination, creating a close bond and understanding of each other's needs between writer and pet through the long hours spent together.

The feline-featured French writer Colette (1873–1954) with her beloved Chartreux cats, in a moment of reflection.

A kitten who becomes a writer's muse may initially regard the pen or pencil as a plaything, but it soon learns that its role is to be a source of inspiration and a gentle recipient of doubts and queries. Sometimes feline muses appear to be inspired themselves, such as Théophile Gautier's white cat, Don Pierrot de Navarre, who often grabbed the pen as though seized by a desire to write. The game of intercepting the moving carriage of a typewriter gives a nasty pinch to inquisitive paws and is soon relinquished – these days the ubiquitous computer does not seem to hold the same fascination. Cats make good paperweights, though they have an uncanny habit of guarding too fiercely the most valuable and frequently used reference sources. However, although they dislike being pestered, cats hate being completely ignored even more, and attentive stroking

33

A cat makes a perfect writer's companion as in this portrait of an unknown sitter (sometimes identified as Pierre Loti) by Henri Rousseau.

ensures that the writer does not overdo things and develop repetitive strain injury. It also keeps the muse firmly in place.

In addition to being literary midwives, many authors' cats also appear in their masters' work. The Czech playwright Karel Capek kept dozens of cats, many of which he wrote about. He records how, on the same day that he was mourning the loss of one of his favourite pets, a stray female cat appeared on his doorstep.

He adopted her, and named her Pudlenka, and she subsequently produced 26 kittens, one of whom, Pudlenka II, also had 21 kittens of her own. A third generation cat from this extensive family, Pudlenka III, went on to produce so many offspring that Capek felt they could "rule the universe" – they were certainly a major force in his world.

Cleveland Amory, founder of the Fund for Animals, has written three best-sellers about his cat Polar Bear, the white stray he found injured one snowy Christmas Eve, while British publisher Michael Joseph wrote about his cat Charles, and a shorthaired tortoiseshell tabby called Minna Minna Mowbray whom he considered to have an outstanding personality. Another British writer whose feelings for the cats in her life spill out onto the written page, is Zimbabwean-born novelist Doris Lessing, who has written about her cats in both Africa and England with great affection.

Many French authors have celebrated their feline friends. As well as Théophile

Gautier, they include Alexandre Dumas, who formed a Feline Defence League with fellow novelists Guy de Maupassant and Anatole France, and the cat-besotted poet Charles Baudelaire. Novelist Colette immortalized the imaginary conversations between her gray Angora, Kiki-la Doucette, and her French bulldog, Toby, in *Sept Dialogues de Bêtes* (Seven Animal Dialogues, which was published in English translation as *Barks and Purrs*). Her cats feature in several other of her works and her story entitled *La Chatte* (The Female Cat), about a beautiful Russian Blue whom a young man prefers to his bride, was clearly inspired by her own cat,

36 Saha, who shared her name with the ficitonal cat from the story.

37 A catalogue of cat-loving authors would span centuries and continents to include writers of every genre, ranging from the unknown eighth-century Irish monk who wrote a poem about his companion, Pangur Bán, to Raymond Chandler, who referred to his Persian, Taki, as his "feline secretary". The Brontë sisters had a beloved cat called Tiger, who was much mourned when he died in 1844, **38** while George Sands ate breakfast from the same dish as her cat, Minou, and Edgar Allan Poe worked with his tortoiseshell, Catarina, on his shoulder. French author, artist and film-maker Jean Cocteau dedicated his *Drôle de Ménage* to his cat Karoun, whom he declared to be King of Cats. Cocteau's cats were usually Siamese but it was a gray longhair that inspired the makeup for the beast in his classic movie *Beauty and the Beast*.

39 Charles Dickens was not intially fond of cats and objected when his daughter Mamie's cat, Williamina, having given birth in the kitchen, carried her kittens one by one into his study. When Mamie removed the kittens, Williamina promptly carried them back. Removed again, she brought them to Dicken's feet and with an imploring gaze put them at his mercy. Dickens let Mamie keep only **40** one kitten, but this little girl became his pet and he named her The Master's Cat.

Writer Paul Gallico (shown here with two of his cats) once declared that once a cat has presented its owner with a mouse, the owner will be for ever changed as the cat "can use you for a doormat. And she will too."

"I share the opinion of the Orientals, who rather despise the dog as being tainted with filthy instincts, while they respect and fear the cat as a sort of little sphinx."

from DOGS AND CATS
by Pierre Loti (19th–20th centuries)

"It is the misfortune of cats that they are generally brought into contrast with dogs, whose fidelity, attachment, and sagacity are so often the subjects of admiration. The character of the dog ... would, if viewed in a universal spirit, be open to impeachment. He abandons his kind, and becomes the willing slave and fawning parasite of man. Look if the cat will so far forget her dignity ... for the gratification of man. She is connected with royalty, the head of her family being the lion, King of the Forest. It must be from her relationship that the adage has arisen, 'A cat may look at a king.' "

from INTERESTING ANECDOTES OF THE ANIMAL KINGDOM
by Thomas Brown (1834)

Artists' Cats

As cats tend to be beautiful creatures, we would expect them to be a favourite subject for artists, but, in Western art at least, they did not become a major focus for painting until comparatively recent times. In medieval and early-Renaissance art they sometimes had a symbolic presence but they first started to

Cats feature only as the occasional accessory in the work of French artist Henri Matisse (1869–1954), but this black cat was his devoted companion, especially in the years when he was ill and often confined to bed.

LEFT *This self-portrait of Japanese artist Tsugouhara Foujita shows something of the close bond that he had with cats.*

appear on a larger scale in the later seventeenth-century Dutch and eighteenth-century French genre paintings of domestic scenes.

Some of the greatest artists from the Renaissance onward sketched and painted cats, including Leonardo da Vinci, who declared that "even the smallest feline is a work of art," Michelangelo Buonarroti, Paolo Veronese and Pieter Breughel, but we do not know if the models they used were their own pets. In 1526, Francesco Umbertini painted a rare portrait of a young woman with a cat, but neither of the sitters' names are known, while around the middle of the sixteenth century, Bassano and other artist members of his family, painted pictures featuring a particular feline and it is tempting to speculate that this cat is either the same family pet or several similar-looking relatives.

In later years cats began to appear more widely in art. There are some Dutch paintings of cats fighting or raiding larders, and, although there are delightful instances of cats shown with children or young women, there are only a few paintings, such as Goya's portrait of Don Manuel, son of the Count of Altamira, or William Hogarth's depiction of the Graham children, that we know for sure portray the subjects' pets.

The first artist to make cats his major subject was Gottfried Mind, a Hungarian-born painter who lived in Berne, Switzerland, in the eighteenth century. Although contemporaries dubbed him "the Raphael of Cats," to modern eyes his pictures look stilted and neither his skill nor

Foss, the beloved cat of British artist and writer Edward Lear (1812–1888), is shown here in a drawing by Lear himself. When Lear moved home during Foss's twilight years, he had a new house built just like the old one so that the cat would know its way around.

powers of observation rate this comparison – but there can be no doubt that he idolized cats. Mind's favourite cat was called Minette and he used to hold long conversations with her while he worked. When, in 1809, an outbreak of rabies led the Berne authorities to order the destruction of all cats in the city, he hid her and she was saved, though he was heartbroken at the loss of so many others.

Mind's successor as the leading cat artist was Dutch-born Henrietta Ronner, one of a number of skilled animal painters of the Victorian period. Her scenes of cats and kittens and of dog-cat confrontations are well observed, if a little sentimental, and clearly show her affection for the cat. So, too, do the lively drawings, lithographs and posters of Théophile Steinlen, a Swiss artist who worked in Paris from the 1890s. He would take his sketchbook out into Montmartre to capture images of the street cats – cats patrolling the rooftops or raiding garbage bins – as well as painting artists' and seamstresses' pets in more conventional settings. His reputation as a cat-lover soon spread and his house, with all its feline inhabitants, came to be known as Cats' Corner.

It was not just in the West, however, that cats became a popular subject for artists. During the 1700s, on the other side of the world, the Edo studio of Utagawa Kuniyoshi was always full of cats and kittens which frequently feature in the work of this master of Japanese woodcuts.

Another Japanese cat specialist was Tsugouharu Foujita, who settled in Paris in 1913. He made many studies of felines, even including a favourite cat in self-portraits. Foujita was a good friend of Picasso, whose painted cats usually appear as savage predators but whose own pet cats included at least one elegant Siamese. English painter Gwen John also lived in France, and she could never abandon a cat. After taking her pet, Tiger, to visit her lover who lived in the country, the cat suddenly dashed off the tramcar at St Cloud, on the journey back to Paris. She desperately tried to find him, sleeping rough for six nights before returning,

catless, to Paris. When a message arrived that Tiger had been seen, Gwen returned to spend another three nights outside before he reappeared.

Even better known as a cat lover is Louis Wain, an English artist whose kitten Peter sat for Wain's first cat portrait. However, Wain gradually became madly obsessive about cats and increasingly abandoned oil-painting for cartoon-like illustrations, often showing cats clothed and accoutred like people and transposed into human situations. Today, his work tends to produce reactions of either great delight or extreme distaste, but it was undoubtedly popular around the turn of the twentieth century. He was also actively involved in the world of cats and even became President of the National Cat Club.

English artist George Stubbs (1724–1806) is famous for his animal paintings, but this is his only known portrait of an individual cat – a kitten, who is identified as the pet of a certain Miss Anne White.

Cats and other Creatures

For centuries dogs were regarded as loyal and affectionate, earning them the epithet "man's best friend", whereas cats were seen as, at best, useful mousers and at worst, evil witches' familiars. In fact, both dog and cat behaviour toward humans is a reflection of their biological backgrounds – the dog is constantly displaying subservience to his "pack leader" and the more independent and apparently aloof cat is being true to its solitary nature. As dogs and cats have

This painting, Beyond the Ilex by 20th-century, American artist Derold Page, shows a cat surrounded by its natural prey, but cats can learn to live in harmony with birds and other animals, sometimes even rearing orphans of other species.

evolved such contrasting behaviour in the wild, it is hardly surprising that they are traditional antagonists in the domestic environment, but although their differences may provoke a measure of reserve in cat-dog relations, reared together, dogs and cats can prove devoted companions – often with the cat calling all the shots.

A cat called Hinse dominated the dogs in the household of novelist Sir Walter Scott but one day a young bloodhound, who was fed up with being bullied, snapped back a little too strongly and put an end to Hinse's reign. Such an incident could never have happened between grey-furred Pepper and his friend,

Teddy the Great Dane. They appeared in many movies with Charlie Chaplin and the Keystone Cops and when eventually Teddy died Pepper was disconsolate.

Female cats have often raised orphan animals of other species such as rabbits, squirrels, rats and mice, which are their natural prey, and even ducks and chickens. This reflects the cat's strong mothering instinct but can hardly explain some of the more unusual feline friendships, such as that of American President Calvin Coolidge's cat Timmie with a canary.

There could hardly be two more unlikely companions than the elephant and the cat that Mark Twain discovered on a visit to the Zoological Gardens in Marseilles, France. The cat would climb up the elephant's legs and settle on his back to sun herself throughout the afternoon. They became firm buddies and the cat used to run aloft to safety at any sign of danger, completely secure in the elephant's protection.

Another unlikely bond was formed at the Gorilla Foundation, in California, between Koko, a female gorilla, and a kitten. Sadly, the kitten was run over, but Koko was soon presented with another tiny ginger Manx. The gorilla was delighted with her new friend and, having learned a large vocabulary of signs with which to communicate with humans, she told her keepers that she had named the kitten Lips-Lipstick: "My cat good," she signalled.

Cats by *Night*

Cats are nocturnal creatures, or at least crepuscular ones – that is, they are most active at dusk and just before dawn. This observation led the ancients to link them with goddesses of the moon and the night, and hence later Christian lore linked them with witches and demons. While cats hunt during the day, too, and they certainly do not prowl around all night long – they sleep too many hours for that – night is definitely the time of the cat.

In his poem "The Cat and the Moon", the Irish poet W.B. Yeats tells of Minnaloushe, "the nearest kin to the moon", as she creeps stealthily through the moonlight.

This Egyptian papyrus of the 12th century BCE, shows the sun-god Ra, in cat form, striking the head of Apopis, the serpent of the night, to ensure that the dawn will return.

The caterwauling cat on the tiles, who disturbs the night, is an altogether less romantic character. The way in which cats congregate at night and "sing" together inspired Heinrich Heine to write in his poem *The Young Cats' Club for Poetry-Music*: "O what a croaking, snarling and noise!/O what mewing and yelling," topped by a cat called Sontag "languid and shrieking". Most of the caterwauling that wakes you up is the sound of cat courtship but Heine's gatherings do happen. In areas where there is a substantial domestic cat population outside at night, male cats gather, usually on a roof or patch of ground that is outside the personal territory of any particular cat. There they groom each other, vocalize and indeed socialize much like people at a party, with rarely any aggression. This phenomenon has even been called night "clubbing".

Pet cats whose lives are closely intertwined with those of their keepers, especially cats who are not free to roam outside, will often adapt their daily routine to match that of their owner. Such cats prefer to spend the night curled up on a bed than to go out on the tiles. For one young writer, during a bitter British winter in an unheated, freezing room, a warm bundle of black fur beneath the covers kept the perils of frostbite at bay. Sharing body-heat for mutual warmth is natural behaviour in such circumstances, but this cat burrowed deeply into the bed and deliberately chose to snuggle around its keeper's feet.

In this painting, Erskine Returning at Dawn, *by the artist Tirzah Ravilious, the cat comes home as the sun comes up, because the best times for hunting are lost with the daylight.*

Predators and Scavengers

It was the cat's usefulness and not its potential as a companion that originally assured its place beside us in the home, with the most frequently asked question by a possible owner being: "Is it a good mouser?" Its highly-attuned senses and hunter's physique make the cat a truly formidable mouse-catcher.

In the wild cats feed mainly on mice and voles but their diet may include birds, rabbits, small reptiles, shrews, butterflies, fish and even snakes, depending on the surrounding habitat. Cats also eat grass, which provides roughage and acts

as an emetic to bring up the balls of fur they have swallowed when grooming.

Living with humans has acquainted domesticated felines with a wide variety of vegetables and grain-based foods, and we are responsible for introducing them to such strange and sophisticated tastes as cheese and chocolate. However, as cats are essentially carnivores, they must have meat in their diet – without the amino acid taurine, they will go blind, and they cannot manufacture fatty acids or absorb Vitamin A from vegetables.

LEFT *Cats are never completely domesticated – they always retain their hunter's instincts. This Roman mosaic from the 1st century* CE *shows a successful hunter with a bird.*

Watch a kitten at play and you see a hunter in the making – practising the rudiments of stalking, ambushing and pouncing. Of course, not all felines become master hunters. Any cat who aspires to be a top mouser has to beat the record established by a Scottish cat called Towser, who was employed at the Glenturret whisky distillery on Tayside. Born in Scotland's oldest operational distillery, Towser caught an average of three mice a day – a grand total of 28,899 – until dying in service in 1987.

The story of Tibbald the cat, by the fourteenth-century Persian poet Obaid-e Zakani, perfectly illustrates the cat's predatory nature. Having killed a mouse, a repentant Tibbald offers to make amends to all its surviving relatives. Trusting that he has truly reformed, they come to him to collect their compensation only to be mercilessly killed and devoured. When the two survivors escape and report the tyrant to the authorities, an army of mice catches Tibbald, who is tried and condemned – but he still manages to outwit them all, and even swallows the judge as he makes his escape.

Few people are upset if a cat catches a mouse or a rat, but a bird is a different matter. In fact birds form a very small proportion of the feline diet, though this may owe more to the birds' ability to escape than to any preference on the part of cats!

RIGHT *A cat with fastidious table manners selects a tasty morsel from the diner's plate in* The Checked Blouse, *a painting by Pierre Bonnard (1867–1947). This is truly domestic hunting!*

The predatory nature of the cat is revealed in all its stark reality in Cat with a Bird in its Jaws, *painted by Pablo Picasso (1881–1973).*

Many poets, from the Byzantine Agathias to modern-day Stevie Smith, have written about bird predation. The sixteenth-century poet John Skelton is very wrathful at the murder of his sparrow Phillip by his cat Gyb: "That vengeaunce I aske and crye,/By way of exclamacyon,/On all the hole nacyon/Of cattes wylde and take/God send them sorowe and shame!/That cat specyally,/That slew so cruelly/My lytell pretty sparowe/That I brought up at Carowe!"

48

This illustration from the 14th-century Luttrell Psalter shows a playful medieval cat toying with a hapless rat.

Of course, Gyb was only following his instincts and could not have predicted his master's ire. Making allowances for the cat's true nature also saved Alexandre Dumas's pet, Mysouff, from dire punishment when he was discovered one morning in the aviary, having eaten all the birds. Cats, however, sometimes have the tables turned on them. In one example, Théophile Gautier's cat, Madame Théophile, was about to pounce on the pet parrot, when the well-trained bird asked her (in a perfect imitation of a human voice), "Have you had your breakfast?" Shocked by the talking bird, the intrepid hunter lost her nerve and darted to take cover beneath a bed. Poor, terrified Madame Théophile refused to come out for a whole day!

In some cases cats have been appreciated for their bird hunting. Sir Henry Wyat, a prisoner in the Tower of London in the sixteenth century, is reputed to have made friends with a cat, who not only frequented his dungeon and curled up to share her warmth with him, but regularly caught pigeons for his supper.

Most cats relish the exciting chase of the hunt, but many are also shamelessly opportunistic and will rarely turn down an effortless meal. If someone chooses to leave a tasty snack unattended, it would be almost churlish of the crafty animal to ignore it, and taking the food in such circumstances can hardly be deemed stealing. At Mediterranean outdoor restaurants it is not uncommon to see the local cats sizing up the soft touches among the tourists, and waiting until the waiters' backs are turned before darting in to beg for food with all the pathos and polished performance of accomplished actors.

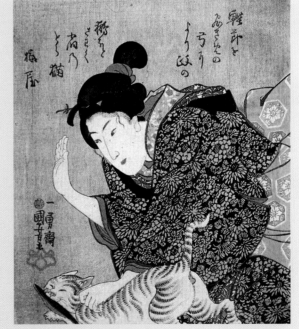

A girl chastises a cat who has just raided the larder in this Japanese woodblock by Kuniyoshi (c. 1845).

Cats that Fish

These cats seem captivated by the proximity of such tantalizing prey in White Cats Watching Goldfish, *by Arthur Heyer (1872–1931).*

According to a medieval Latin proverb "the cat likes fish to eat but hates to wet her feet," but some enterprising cats manage to get around this problem. Cats do not hate water in general – just unexpected wetness – and they are perfectly happy dipping a paw into liquid and then licking it, say, to reach the cream at the bottom of a jug. Kittens at play will often use a special technique to flip things into the air and it is this action that gives cats the ability to fish.

There are many examples of adventurous cats who overcame their dislike of both water and cold for the sake of their fish supper. At Devil's Point naval battery in Plymouth, southern England, a cat plunged daily into the sea and then presented her catch to the sailors in the guard room. A choosy Australian cat used to sit on a jetty for hours, waiting for its favourite mullet to come within range. In 1829, a cat belonging to a Mr Moody of Jesmond in the north of England was seen teaching a neighbour's cat to fish successfully; and the naturalist Charles Darwin noted how cats dart into shallow water to fish. One of Russian composer Alexander Borodin's many cats was a tabby called Rybolov (meaning "fisherman") because he had developed the skill of fishing through holes in the winter ice. In Paris, France, there is even a street – the rue du Chat qui Pêche (the "street of the fishing cat") – named after a seventeenth-century cat who caught fish from cellars following a flood of the River Seine.

Less adept was one of the English writer Horace Walpole's cats, Selima, a tortoiseshell tabby who fell into a tub of goldfish and drowned – probably as a result of exhaustion, for cats swim instinctively, it is just that they need to have the energy to find somewhere to climb out. One cat that particularly enjoyed a regular dip was Ariel, a cat belonging to Carl van Vechten – it would leap into his owner's bath each morning for a swim.

A Cat with Trout, Perch and Carp on a Ledge, *attributed to the late-18th-century artist Stephen Elmer. This cat has been blessed with a good find rather than a good catch and knows we should never look a gift fish in the mouth.*

"A cat caught a sparrow, and was about to
devour it, but the sparrow said, 'No gentleman
eats till he has first washed his face.'
The cat, struck with this remark, set the
sparrow down and began to wash his face with
his paw, but the sparrow flew away. This vexed
Pussy extremely, and he said, 'As long as I live I
will eat first and wash my face afterward.'
Which all cats do, even to this day."

from THE BOOK OF CATS: A CHIT-CHAT CHRONICLE
by Charles H. Ross (1868)

Cats on Location

Cats in the city must be fiercely territorial, while cats
in the country can live more freely, choosing huge
barns and whole fields as "theirs". By looking at
cats in situ *we gain new insights into their*
characteristics, as well as a new perspective on
and feeling for place. But, above all, as the English
painter Stanley Spencer once wrote, "Wherever
a cat sits, there shall happiness be found."

City Cats

Cats are very versatile creatures and long ago they found many ways of adapting to city life. The dapper cats of fiction, such as Balzac's well-fed and well-groomed cats-about-town in his *Love Life of an English Cat*, may represent the lucky few who live at smart addresses – although many such cats find themselves little more than prisoners in their comfortable homes.

The life of the alley cat is a very different story. There are examples of such street cats in the poems of T.S. Eliot, on which the British composer Andrew Lloyd Webber based his famous musical *Cats* – such as Macavity "the master criminal who can defy the law" and the waif Grizabella, a former "glamour cat", who reminisces about happier times under the lamplight. But the queen of all alley cats must be the inimitable mehitabel (sic), who was invented by New York columnist Don Marquis and immortalized by her friend Archie the cockroach who could not reach the shift key on the typewriter to make capital letters. Archie believes "that formerly her spirit/was incarnated in the body of/cleopatra/that was a long time ago/and one must not be/surprised if mehitabel/has forgotten some of her/more regal manners."

Feral city cats have to be opportunists. They may catch a mouse or rat but mostly they survive by scavenging and on handouts from people who are kind enough to feed them. There are feral cats in the excavated ruins of ancient Rome and Athens, and in the traffic-free piazzas of Venice, but these city cats mainly frequent any railed-off area – say, around an institutional building, such as a hospital or a public utility, where the high fences may offer them protection from marauding dogs and other enemies.

Colonies of city cats can grow to considerable numbers. English cat expert Roger Tabor studied one such group in a London square. They were fed regularly by a number of volunteers so that Tabor could determine which cats ate most of the food and which were prepared to share their food with others.

Ruskin Spear, a British artist of the 20th century, recorded typical urban scenes in his paintings. This piece, entitled Top Cat, *shows an archetypal city scavenger prowling the trash for his next meal.*

Country Cats

Some country cats are feral but most are usually attached to human settlements even if they are not living as household pets. They are important on farms to control rodents, and often make their homes in barns and other outbuildings where mice and rats are readily found as prey.

Working farm cats live a very different life from pampered city pets. They are usually more self-sufficient, living as hunters and scavengers, although many will be provided with milk or other supplementary food. Contrary to popular belief, feeding a cat does not discourage it from hunting – indeed evidence shows that ensuring cats have enough basic food to stay fit and healthy is the best way to keep them effective as rodent catchers.

Cat populations are not nearly as dense in the country as in towns or cities, so rural territories are usually more extensive. Females tend to live close together, whereas toms have ranges which overlap those of several females. A study by John Laundré in Wisconsin showed that females used farm buildings for both resting and hunting while males roamed much farther afield. Farm buildings may become the base for a colony of cats who live fairly harmoniously, although there is usually a pecking order, often based on the supremacy of a mother over her daughters and other descendants.

Country cats, like this handsome tom in Timothy Easton's Predators, *have less competition for territory than their urban counterparts. They also often have the best of all worlds – barns full of mice, trees full of birds and acres of space in which to prowl or doze in the sunshine.*

An urban cat who moves to the countryside probably finds it much easier to establish a territory than a rural cat does in a town or city. Mandy, the black longhaired cat belonging to actor Sandor Eles, grew up in a town. Her world was limited to his apartment and patio, enclosed on all sides by high walls. However, when Sandor took time off from television and the movies to spend the summer acting at the Festival Theatre in Pitlochry, Scotland, Mandy rapidly adapted to living in a remote cottage in the Highlands, using her urban sophistication to learn to ride pillion on her keeper's motor scooter. She seemed to have no competition for territory but it was pure instinct that made this cat, who had previously never so much as caught a mouse, explore the mountainside, catching and killing rabbits bigger than herself to bring home for her keeper.

Cats at Work

You may not expect your cat to "earn" its keep, but many cats are kept as working animals and some of them have even been put on an official payroll! Undoubtedly, the greatest and most popular job for a cat is chief mouser. Nini, a large white tomcat, became a great friend of regulars at a coffee shop in Venice, Italy, in the 1890s. Moonlighting from his day job as mouser at the café, Nini would regularly make the short journey to the Venetian State Archive, where he would take a nap and act as a deterrent to stop mice nibbling the

This painting (c.1820), by an anonymous artist, shows a cat preparing to ambush a mouse. The wide eyes and stiffly upright ears are characteristic of a cat about to pounce on its prey.

This detail from a 13th-century bestiary is testimony to the long-standing tradition that a cat's primary work is as a mouser.

papers. He also regularly called in at the Frari church and so gained a reputation for being both devout and learned. A visitors' book, kept by the church and signed by his admirers, included entries by a pope, a tzar, a king and queen of Italy, and, most famously, the composer Giuseppe Verdi who even added a few notes from his opera *La Traviata*.

Archive and library work has been a popular occupation for cats for thousands of years. There are records of their participation going back as far as the earliest Christian monasteries and the temples of the Far East, where precious scrolls needed protection from the ravages of mice. More recently, between 1908 and 1929, scholars from all over the world met Mike, the museum cat in the British Library. Mike was introduced to the museum as a kitten, by the resident reading-room cat, Black Jack, who one day dropped him at the feet of the Keeper of Egyptian Antiquities. As Mike grew up he began to share the duties of the museum's gatekeeper. Taking himself and his job very seriously, he would allow only the gatekeeper and the Egyptologist to stroke or pet him –

This turn-of-the-century illustration of Puss-in-Boots by Osswald von Eugen demonstrates the devious nature of the working cat. He may be a character from folklore but there is nothing fictional about feline wiliness!

maintaining the utmost professionalism with other members of staff. Apart from mousing, Mike entrapped the pigeons that fouled the museum grounds. He would catch one and take it, wings flapping, to the museum staff, who would give him a titbit and let the pigeon go. His like is sorely needed to keep away the pigeons today, but sadly there is no cat currently employed there.

Mousing and pest control have not been the only occupations for which cats have proven useful. Smudge, a handsome black-and-white cat, was a much-loved resident at the People's Palace, a museum and social centre in Glasgow, Scotland. A fully paid-up Trade Union member, he also modelled for porcelain statues of himself to sell to tourists.

58

Traditionally, post offices have also been common places to find working cats. Tommy, of Hartford, Connecticut, was an American post office cat. He extended his skills by learning tricks, which he performed for an enthusiastic audience at a benefit concert in order to raise money for mailmen. Another cat, Fang, a heavyweight white longhair, served the community of Grand Prairie, Texas, as the official police cat, and had his own ID, complete with photograph.

Ancient Egyptian pictures of marshland hunting scenes, like this wallpainting from the 1400-BCE tomb of Nebaum, suggest that the Egyptians may have trained cats as retrievers.

Railroads, too, have long-serving cats but none perhaps as substantial as Tiddles, a tabby-and-white 32-pounder (14.5kg). He was the only male allowed in the ladies' restroom at London's Paddington Station in the 1970s. Tiddles, who had his own fan club, was taken home once by the lady in charge but he did not like being away from his station and his comfortable napping-place in a corner in the restroom.

59

Back in 1867, Joseph Cave, the new manager of London's Old Vic Theatre, was dismayed to find it overrun with rats. Deciding against the use of poison, he found a half-starved "rowdy-looking brindled feline" and enticed it into the theatre to take over rodent control. The cat then recruited a friend who was also put on the payroll and before long the theatre had 20 cats! Probably the longest-serving theatre cat was Beerbohm, a sturdy tabby, who was born in Her Majesty's Theatre, London. He took up a position at the Globe

60

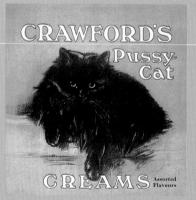

CRAWFORD'S Pussy-Cat

CREAMS Assorted Flavours

Cats have often been used as marketing aids – their images have helped to sell products of many kinds, from cookies and milk to more obscure products, such as railway services.

Theatre, London, at the beginning of the 1970s, working there for 20 years until his retirement to the theatre carpenter's home where he died in 1995.

Some cats are drawn to perform in the glamorous world of the arts. Feedback, for example, at the radio station WJCO in Jackson, Michigan, not only kept mice out of the machinery but often went on air too with a personal greeting to all listeners. Then there are the feline circus artists, actors, film stars and those who earn their keep giving their personal endorsement to cat foods. In Britain, Arthur, a white cat, became a household name from starring in a series of advertisements for a well-known brand of canned food. In the

USA, Morris, a large ginger tom, started life modestly in a Chicago animal shelter and went on to visit the White House and star in a Hollywood movie. However, the highlight of his career came when he won a special "Patsy" – the animal version of an Oscar – for his work in commercials. More famous even than Morris was another ginger cat called Orangey, who twice won a Patsy – first for his role in *Rhubarb* in 1951 and then for appearing in *Breakfast at Tiffany's* ten years later. He also regularly appeared on television.

On a more serious note, the incredible occupation of a cat called Mourka during World War II was far removed from Hollywood luxury, although no less exciting and perhaps far more admirable. During the Battle of Stalingrad, Mourka risked life and limb in order to carry messages regarding enemy positions from a group of Russian scouts back to their headquarters. Other felines may have an easier life but dedication to duty, such as that shown by Mourka, is the hallmark of the working cat.

Artist Théophile Steinlen, famous for his cat paintings, often made felines a feature of his pictures for advertisements, such as this one for sterilized milk.

"To the rats in the barn he's a tiger,
The field mice are scared of his claws
But for me he's a cuddly bundle
Who always has velvety paws."

Anonymous (20th century)

"The cat of slums and alleys ... still keeps, amid the prowlings of its adversity, the old, free, pantherlike tread with which it paced of yore the temple courts of Thebes; still displays the self-reliant watchfulness which man has never taught it to lay aside."

from THE SQUARE EGG
by Hector Hugo Munro (Saki; 1870–1916)

Cats at Sea

Although cats have a reputation for hating water, they have an extensive seafaring history. A few privileged cats have had the opportunity to travel as passengers on ships, such as the much-loved pet of Francisco Mori, a seventeenth-century Doge of Venice, but most cats at sea are working animals. During the thirteenth century, European crusaders inadvertently brought back to their homelands new breeds of rats. These hardy vermin were responsible for the bubonic plague, often known as the Black Death, which devastated Europe during the fourteenth century. Cats proved themselves efficient at keeping down the rodent population and good mariners, so they soon became regular crew members on both mechant and naval vessels.

In a British children's story, the only possession of a poor young man, Dick Whittington, is a cat. Arriving in London to seek his fortune, Dick loans the cat as a mouser to a ship about to depart on a trading voyage. The story goes that the cat clears the ship of a plague of rats and earns Dick a fortune. Dick Whittington was real – he became Lord Mayor of London three times in the late fourteenth and early fifteenth centuries – but the inclusion of a cat in the story comes from the influence of a folktale with similar themes, occuring across several cultures. However, the tale does emphasize the importance of a ship's cat.

A sixteenth-century Italian ship, the *Fila Caverna*, was sailing from Venice to Jerusalem when the ship's cat was blown overboard. Luckily the sailors spotted her swimming, her head bobbing above the water despite the huge waves, and the captain ordered a boat to be rowed back half a mile to rescue her. In more recent times there was a ship's cat, which during World War II, managed to serve on both sides in the conflict. Oscar began his naval career with the German Navy as mascot of the German battleship, the *Bismarck*, which sank the British battleship *HMS Hood* and then was herself torpedoed and sunk outside the French port of Brest. Oscar escaped but could not have survived long swimming among the wreckage if he had not been hauled out by a British sailor who took him back to *HMS Cossack*. Only five months later this destroyer, too, was sunk but Oscar was again among the survivors and continued his career on *HMS Ark Royal* until she was destroyed by a U-boat. By now Oscar was an accomplished swimmer, but once the *Ark Royal* had gone down and Oscar was rescued again,

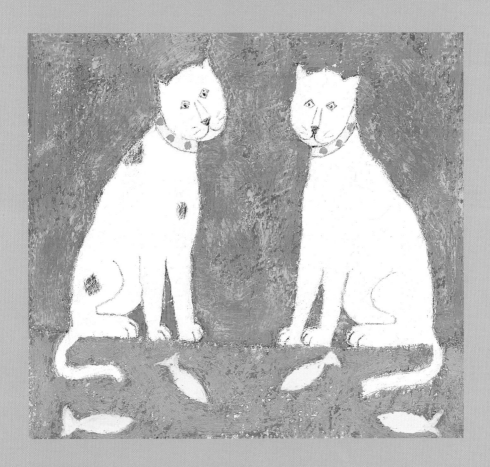

The saki-*drinking cats in* The Cat's Voyage *by contemporary Japanese artist Ryozo Kohira, are sailing out to sea, leaving Mount Fuji in the distance.*

the British authorities decided he had already used up too many of his nine lives and retired him from service.

A few years later, in 1949, in a confrontation between the Royal Navy's *HMS Amethyst* and Chinese communist forces on the Yangtse River, a Hong-Kong-born ship's cat Simon came under fire. A shell killed an officer in the captain's cabin and wounded the black-and-white tom but he did not let this incident interrupt his duties.

In 1975, when the Royal Navy decided that it was proving too difficult to enforce the UK's strict quarantine laws (it is not easy to ensure that no cat descends the gangplank in foreign ports) cats were banned from Her Majesty's ships. However, they were permitted to continue their official duties on shore. Charlie, service number C1111115, held his own Navy pay book at Chatham shore base. Unfortunately, at only one year old, he was run over, having had little chance to play his part in naval history.

Do feline sailors share the reputation of other seamen of having "a girl in every port"? Mark Twain certainly thought so. When travelling on the *SS Oceana*, which boasted three adult cats and a basket of kittens, he reported that there was one that went ashore at every port "to see how his various families are getting along" and then was not seen again until the ship was ready to sail. His shipmates thought that he checked out the dock each day: the bustle of arriving passengers and baggage being loaded, indicated when it was time to go aboard.

Seafarers the world over have held a variety of superstitions about cats. Generally it was thought propitious to have a cat aboard a boat – although some thought it unlucky to say the word "cat" – perhaps because of the punishment inflicted on many of them by the "cat-o'-nine-tails" (a vicious whip with nine leather straps). Japanese sailors were convinced that a sure way to drive the storm devils away was to get a tortoiseshell cat to climb up the rigging to the top of the mast.

Cats of Egypt

In ancient Egypt the cat was a sacred beast worshipped in temples, treated with kindness and respect, and mummified after death. The small cat was originally considered a manageable version of its larger cousins, but eventually it was venerated in its own right as the goddess Bastet, a deity of the moon, fertility and protection. One papyrus painting even shows the sun-god Ra in cat form decapitating the serpent of darkness to symbolize the victory of night over day.

In the tomb of Theban harbourmaster May, c.1450BCE, a wall painting shows a ginger cat wearing a collar, beneath the chair of May's wife, Tui.

96

Cats became so important to ancient Egyptians that anyone who harmed them was severely punished. In the century before the birth of Christ, a Roman visitor to Egypt had the misfortune to accidentally kill a cat. He was saved from being lynched only because he was on a diplomatic mission.

Egyptian reverence for the cat goes back some four-and-a-half-thousand years. One of the most important gods of ancient Egypt, the cat-goddess Bastet began life as a lioness deity. At around 900BCE, in the city of Bubastis on the Nile Delta, King Osorkon built a new hypostyle hall in Bastet's temple. At roughly the same time, Bastet's image evolved to look more like a domestic cat than a lioness. Consequently, statues of her usually depict a woman with a cat's head, or an elegantly carved cat with kittens around her feet, to emphasize her role as a fertility deity. Bubastis (meaning the "city of Bastet") soon became one of the major religious centres of Lower Egypt, and was a place of annual pilgrimage for thousands of people from all over the country, who sailed down the Nile for an orgiastic celebration in Bastet's honour. At the inner courts of the temple complex, the real but sacred cats of the goddess were looked after by priests whose office was passed down from father to son.

Among the ruling classes of ancient Egypt cats may have been kept as pets, as they were believed to bring good fortune and prosperity to the household. Wall paintings in ancient tombs show cats and kittens sitting under chairs and on laps, just as they do in our own homes today. However, some experts have suggested that these and other cats in Egyptian tomb paintings are intended only as symbols – that is, they do not represent real scenes or real animals. As well as being a symbolic representation of good luck, the cat was also regarded as a talisman to ensure the fertility and hence rebirth of the dead into the afterlife.

According to some scholars, when an Egypitan pet cat died, household members shaved off their eyebrows and went into mourning (the eyebrows represented the cat's fur). The cat was then embalmed, mummified and offered for burial. The mummified cat shown here dates from between 664 and 332BCE.

On the walls of the tomb of the sculptor Nabumen, a hunting scene depicts a cat among papyrus stalks with wildfowl in its mouth and claws. Nabumen himself is shown punting through the marshland of the Nile Delta, a throwing stick in his hand, and accompanied by his wife. While the cat was regarded as a good omen for Nabumen's rebirth after death, this symbolism does not necessarily conflict with the more obvious interpretation that the cat was his domestic pet. Some experts suggest that the cat shown in this particular wall painting, as well as in others like it, is a retriever – that is, it was trained to bring back fowl after the birds had been brought down by throwing sticks. If this is the case, then it seems likely that the ancient Egyptians kept cats as working pets.

Although Bastet was Egypt's main religious link between cats and divinity, ancient Egyptian painting often places representations of the cat alongside other important symbols and gods in the belief system. The famous eye of Horus (the *wedjat*, meaning "whole one") is sometimes depicted surrounded by images of cats. It was believed that the *wedjat* was all-seeing, and we may speculate that the Egyptians believed the cat to be so keenly connected with the gods that it too held insight into things unseen by the human eye. This would certainly

This Egyptian tomb painting (First Dynasty, c.3000–2800BCE), shows cats herding geese. Both animals were associated with the sun and sky by the ancient Egyptians, so the cat may represent the rising sun or, more probably, the rebirth of souls into the afterlife.

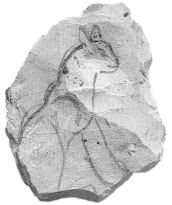

explain why, much later, cats were thought to be psychic and to have magic powers. The Egyptian lunar goddess Isis, Horus's mother, was also associated with cats. Again, medieval European tradition parallels this belief by closely linking the cat and the moon.

The cult of the cat remained a major feature of Egyptian life right up to the Roman period, when the mythology surrounding this sacred animal began to spread across the Mediterranean Sea into Europe and beyond. Officially, however, people were not permitted to take cats out of Egypt – it was intended that these living representatives of Bastet should remain in the country where their goddess was sacred. Nevertheless, some were smuggled out and the domestic cat embarked on its gradual colonization of the rest of the world.

Egyptian cats continued to be highly coveted for their striking aesthetic qualities. When the Princess Natalie Troubetskoy came across two genuine Egyptian cats belonging to the Egyptian Ambassador in Rome, Italy, in the early twentieth century, she was so struck by their beauty that she vowed to create a breed that would emulate the sacred ancestors of ancient times. She borrowed the ambassador's tomcat, Geppo, and then arranged to import a female kitten from Cairo, which she named Baba. The princess mated the two cats and Baba dutifully produced a litter of two kittens, though only one – the male kitten Joseph (Jo-Jo) – survived. Undaunted by this setback, the princess went on to mate Jo-Jo successfully with Baba to produce a female kitten, Lisa, the first of a new breed. Princess Natalie called her new line of cats the "Egyptian Mau", and this popular breed still exists today – a slender, alley cat version of a sacred animal from the most ancient civilization in the world.

Siamese Cats

Siamese are thought to have originated from a cross between a Myanmar (Burmese) and a Vietnamese cat during the territorial wars between the two nations in the seventeenth century, and they have been known in Thailand for centuries as one of a range of cats with differing markings that appear in a manuscript known as the *Cat Book Poems*. The most authentic of these proud cats have crossed eyes and kinked tails. Their distinctive eyes are said to have

When Christopher Wood painted his Siamese Cats in 1927, they were already well established as a fashionable breed.

derived from the cat's watchful guardianship over Buddhist temples or sacred ornaments; and the kinked tail, to be the result of its being wrapped around the sacred chalice of the Buddha, or else the lasting sign of a knot tied by a certain princess as an *aide-memoire*. However, over time, the pedigree has gradually been "perfected" and these distinguishing characteristics are now lost. The shadowy "temple" mark that is still found on Siamese today, at the back of the neck, is said to be the print of a god who once picked up the cat with sooty hands.

In Thailand, as elsewhere, the cat was believed to be a vessel of dead souls, especially the souls of deceased kings. Traditionally, a living Siamese cat was placed in the royal tomb with the king's body. Officials then bored a hole into the tomb wall, through which the cat could escape. When the Siamese emerged from the tomb, the king's soul was said to have passed into it and the cat was accorded full royal status with a place at court where it would sit to watch over the new king. When eventually it died, the cat was thought to carry the the dead king's soul to heaven, where it would find him a place among the stars. As recently as 1926, a Siamese cat was present during the coronation of the new King of Siam. As the procession made its way into the palace, the cat was carried alongside the new king in full regal glory.

Siamese cats were shown at the first British cat show in 1871 but it seems that isolated examples were already known in the West. The first Siamese in America was the White House cat, Siam, and the earliest-documented Siamese cats in Britain were a female, Mia, and a male, Pho. They were said to have been a gift to a British Vice Consul from King Chulalongkron (the ruler in the musical *The King and I*), but the story has not been fully authenticated.

This photograph by Jackum Brown shows a Siamese cat in Casablanca, Morocco. First known with brown Seal-point markings, they are now bred in a variety of colours, including both tabby- and tortoiseshell-patterned points.

Cats of the New World

Various feline forms appear in the beliefs and artifacts of pre-Columbian America but there is no evidence that these had any connection with the species from which the domestic cat developed – they are inspired by the native cats of the Americas. There were no known indigenous domestic cats in the New World before the arrival of the Europeans. They could have been introduced by foreign

The huge head in this painting by an unknown American artist might be a symbol of the cat-bird conflict. In Illinois in 1949, a bill restraining cats from hunting birds was presented, but Governor Adlai Stevenson vetoed it, declaring that it was the cat's nature to roam unescorted.

seafarers, or they may have been brought across the Atlantic by the early colonists. Perhaps the first domestic cats of the New World were a litter born and raised on the high seas and the USA just happened to be their first landfall. Unfortunately, we will never know as no surviving personal accounts nor cargo manifests that mention cats have ever been found.

In time, the cats of North America began to develop different characteristics from those of Europe. The Maine Coon, regarded as the oldest American breed, is exceptionally similar to the Norwegian and other longhaired cats, but it is more than likely that it evolved independently and hence similarities are probably pure coincidence. Wild claims about its ancestry have been

made — for example, it is a cross between a wildcat and a racoon, a bobcat or a lynx, but such interbreeding is impossible in nature. Other suggestions involve matings with Angora and other Old World longhaired cats. American shorthairs, which developed later, show a different "type" or physique from European cats, and in recent times some entirely new American breeds have been created.

Settlers kept cats to catch vermin, not as pampered pets, but by the end of the eighteenth century, felines were appreciated for their unique personal qualities, and were no longer regarded merely as rodent controllers. Confederate commander Robert E. Lee was a cat lover. While he was on campaign during the Mexican-American War, he wrote to his daughter asking her to send him a kitten to keep him company.

Minnie, from the Outskirts of the Village is an all-American cat painted by R.P. Thrall — an early 19th-century American artist. Thrall has taken the unusual step of including the cat's name in the title.

"A home without a cat, and a well-fed, well-petted, and properly revered cat, may be a perfect home, perhaps, but how can it prove its title?" In the century since American writer Mark Twain made that declaration, the cat has become firmly established. By 1987, cats outnumbered dogs in American homes and now a quarter of all American adults have a cat.

As well as becoming firm favourites with the common folk, cats have been popular pets with many famous presidents of the USA, including Abraham Lincoln, Theodore Roosevelt and John F. Kennedy. In the Civil War, during Lincoln's visit to General Grant's headquarters, the President discovered three orphan kittens freezing in the winter cold. He rescued them, and gave them a home in the White House where they joined the earliest-recorded First Cat, Tabby, the pet of Tad, Lincoln's son. There may have been earlier feline residents at the White House but if so, there are no references to them.

The next documented White House cat, Siam, was not only First Cat but also the USA's first Siamese. She was a present from the American Consul in Bangkok to Lucy, the wife of President Hayes. After an arduous journey from Thailand to Washington in 1878–9, she created great interest in the breed but sadly fell ill and died only a few months after her arrival. More recently, both Gerald Ford and Jimmy Carter also had Siamese cats at the White House although the cats officially belonged to their daughters.

Theodore Roosevelt had a famous White House cat called Slippers, a bossy gray tabby who came and went as he pleased, often disappearing for days. He is particularly remembered for his behaviour at a diplomatic dinner in 1906 when he chose to stretch himself out on the hall carpet, blocking the way as the guests left the dining room. The President guided the lady he was accompanying to one side of the recumbent cat, and all the other guests had to follow suit, as Slippers was given formal precedence.

Socks, President Bill Clinton's First Cat, takes the podium for an important White House briefing.

After Herbert Hoover in the 1930s, there were no First Cats until the 1961 inauguration of John F. Kennedy. Tom Kitten was really the pet of Kennedy's daughter, Caroline, but his official status was recognized by newsaper obituary notices when he died in 1962. Ronald Reagan kept cats, but since Tom Kitten only First Cat Socks, who arrived with Bill Clinton in 1993, has attracted much interest. Socks, a black-and-white bi-colour named for his white-patched paws, had "his" diary published in 1993 and at one time was receiving 75,000 letters and parcels in fan mail every week.

Cats in High
Places

Cats love to live in the lap of luxury, and many have been very successful in finding favour among some of the world's most powerful leaders to do so. In 884CE, Emperor Koko of Japan was presented with a clever cat which appeared to understand what people said. A century later Emperor Ichijo thought so highly of a kitten called Myobo No Omoto, that he gave her the title of Court Lady of Fifth Rank, as well as a fine red collar, and her own lady-in-waiting.

Cats were highly regarded in China, too. During the Sung Dynasty (960-1279), they appeared in portraits with children of the nobility. Farther west, in France, King Louis XV had a favourite white cat which came to his bed every morning, and played on the table during Councils of State. Other notable cat lovers were Poincaré and Clémenceau, the French heads of state, as well as European leaders such as the German President Paul von Hindenburg and the Russian revolutionary Vladimir Ilyich Lenin.

Britain's Queen Victoria had a longhaired cat called White Heather, and Prime Minister Winston Churchill doted on Nelson, a black

A painting of Henry Wriothesley, third Earl of Southampton, a friend and patron of author William Shakespeare, with his cat in the Tower of London, c. 1601–1603, by John de Critz the Elder. When the Earl was imprisoned, his devoted cat who according to some sources was named Trixie, set out to find him and share his imprisonment.

tom who aided the war effort by serving as Churchill's hot-water bottle at night, so saving fuel. Black-and-white Wilberforce took up duty at Number Ten Downing Street, the official residence of the British Prime Minister, with Edward Heath in 1970 and stayed until he was retired by Margaret Thatcher in the late 1980s. Humphrey, another black-and-white, Downing-Street cat, attracted bad publicity by catching robins in the garden and then disappeared for months. Fortunately, eventually he was found and returned to Number Ten.

Church Cats

Ever since they were worshipped as gods in ancient Egypt, cats have been associated with religion. It is said that the Prophet Mohammed was so taken with his cat, Muezza, that he held it in his arms when he preached in Mecca. In recognition of the Prophet's love of cats, the animals are free to enter mosques as they please and are highly respected by Moslems – to this day it is against Islamic law to kill them. Farther east, cats have been linked with temples since pre-Buddhist days. Apart from keeping the monks company, they were regarded

These cats appear in the Book of Kells, *an Irish manuscript thought to date from the 9th century* CE. *They are shown with mice, suggesting that they would have been kept in monasteries to prevent the rodents from eating precious gospel texts.*

as sacred animals and were believed to carry the souls of the dead.

It is for their links with the monasteries, too, that cats are best known in a Christian context. Twelve hundred years ago an Irish monk copying manuscripts in the monastery at Richenau in Austria wrote a poem about his white cat, Pangur Bán, comparing its life to his. Pangur is not only the first church cat on record but the first pet cat mentioned in European literature. Two centuries earlier, Pope St Gregory the Great, according to his earliest biographer, had a cat as his constant companion during his years as a monk. In the early thirteenth century, a cat was the only domestic animal permitted among an order of English female hermits, and cats are sometimes linked with certain female saints, including St Martha, who is considered to have the welfare of cats in her charge.

With other clerics the cat was not so popular. The early fathers of the Church associated cats with heathen gods and consequently condemned them as devilish. In 1233, Pope Gregory IV issued a Papal Bull declaring them diabolical creatures, and legitimizing the centuries of feline persecution that were to follow. However, despite the ensuing fanatical witchunts and ritual killings of "witches'" cats,

felines still played a useful role controlling vermin in monasteries and churches, and there is a long line of prelates and clergy who were cat lovers.

Cardinal Richlieu, one of the most powerful men in seventeenth-century France, burned witches and their familiars, but delighted in his own pet cats. He had fourteen of them, and each inherited a pension in his will. His favourite, Soumise, often slept on his lap. In England, the cardinal's contemporary Archbishop Laud also liked cats. He was presented with a tabby with a whorl-patterned coat — one of the first of its kind to arrive in Britain. Another cleric, a nineteenth-century Archbishop of Taranto, had three pampered Angora cats named Desdemona, Pantalone and Otello. At mealtimes they were allowed into the dining room where they sat patiently on chairs until they were fed titbits.

Today there are many church cats, but nowhere so many as at the convent of St Nicholas of the Cats, on the Akrotiri peninsular in Cyprus. Cats from Egypt were introduced there in the fourth century to hunt and kill snakes and their descendants still live there today.

This 15th-century Belgian wooden carving on a misericorde, the ledge on which monks could prop themselves during long services, is decorated with a man throwing a cat. It is representative of the attitude of the medieval Christian Church toward cats.

During the temptation of St Francis, the Devil became so frustrated by the monk's resistance that as a last resort he sent a plague of mice to nibble at Francis's clothes and gnaw at his bare feet. However, Francis held his faith and sure enough, as if from nowhere, a cat leapt out and, in what seemed like a terrible rage, attacked and saw off the Devil's mice.

A TRADITIONAL CHRISTIAN FABLE

Cats of Make-believe and Magic

Since ancient times cats have found a place in myth and folklore all over the world, and through the centuries they have been symbols of both the sacred and the profane. In ancient Egypt they were revered as gods; in Europe the onset of Christianity brought with it a suspicion of witches and their familiars. Over time, storytellers and poets have tried to capture on paper the essence of this mysterious creature.

Literary Cats

A woodcut by Raoul Dufy, (1877–1953), for Apollinaire's The Bestiary or Procession of Orpheus. *The cat has been widely celebrated by French writers and artists.*

Literary cats are legion. They feature in Aesop's fables, in fairytales, nursery rhymes and modern children's stories, and cat tales have been popular in most cultures since ancient times, through the Middle Ages, to the present day.

Many writers have immortalized their own pets in essay and memoir, and poets, in particular, have celebrated the cat in all its guises. Felines have taken part in fiction as in life, whether playing a small supporting role in a scene, or contributing a vital element to the plot. Some lucky cats get the leading role and become major protagonists that are central to the narrative.

The cat rose to literary fame in Renaissance Europe. The Spanish poet and dramatist Lope de Vega (1562–1635) wrote a feline epic *The Battle of the Cats*, in which a cat bride is abducted on her wedding day. In the medieval romance of Reynard the Fox, printed by Caxton and famously retold by Goethe, Tybert the Cat is instrumental in bringing Reynard to justice. François Rabelais invented the monstrous cat magistrate Grippeminaud in his *Gargantua and Pantagruel* – a character echoed in La Fontaine's judge Raminagrobis.

Many modern authors have presented us with detective cats. American writers offer Koko in Lilian Braun Jackson's *The Cat Who* books, and Bushy and Pancho who assist in Lydia Adamson's mysteries, while Turkish-born German author Akif Pirinçi in his *Felidae* books presents us with Francis, an articulate cat whose Maine Coon sidekick, Bluebeard, refers to humans as "can-openers". No sleuths manage to catch the murderer cat Ming, killer of his human rival in Patricia Highsmith's *Ming's Biggest Prey*, or the gun-toting cat in Giles Gordon's *The Jealous One*, who shoots his unfaithful keeper at the man's wedding.

Cats not only appear in stories, they also publish them – although a human ghost writer must share the credit. German author E.T.A. Hoffman (whose stories were used in his famous opera) enabled his favourite cat, Murr, to appear in print, while Émile Zola narrates *The Paradise of Cats* for an Angora cat who, jealous of the apparently carefree life of cats he sees out on the roofs, makes a bid for freedom only to realize how much better his life was when he was well-fed and lived in a comfortable home. In *I Am a Cat*, Japanese novelist Soseki Natsume's cat, No-name, not only tells his own story but pokes fun at the pretentiousness of life around him in an English teacher's household. Paul Gallico "translated and edited" *The Silent Meow*, a "manual for kittens, strays and homeless cats" which is full of advice on the best ways to exploit humans. The cat memoir or autobiography has now become almost a genre in itself – in Tom Howard's *The Cat Chronicles*, nine different cats all tell their tales.

Simpkin Housekeeping, (c.1902), an illustration for the Tailor of Gloucester, *by British artist and writer Helen Beatrix Potter (1866–1943).*

Heraldic Cats

In ancient Rome there was a temple dedicated to Liberty, in which the goddess was shown with a cat at her feet. This association with Liberty was probably the reason why several Roman legions incorporated cats in their standards, among them a red cat and a pale-coated cat with a ring-marked tail. Later both the Dutch Republic and the first Republic of Revolutionary France followed the classical precedent and adopted the cat as a symbol of their new-found freedom.

The Vandals and the Suebi, who invaded Gaul and Spain in the fifth century CE, carried the sign of the black cat into battle. Around the same time the kings of Burgundy, France, used a wildcat as an emblem. St Clotilda, a Burgundian princess who became the queen of the Franks, had a black cat killing a rat as her device, set on a gold ground.

As the rules of heraldry developed into a codified system in the Middle Ages, the Christian Church's condemnation of the cat discouraged the animal's use as

an emblem. Nonetheless, there are families whose names derive from the word "cat" and for whom the cat is therefore a most appropriate symbol. Some examples include the German Katzens, who had a crest of a silver cat holding a rat on an azure ground; the Neapolitan Della Gattas, who used a cat couchant; the Chetaldi of Limoges, with two cats argent (silver) on azure; and the English Catesby family's spotted cat. In

ABOVE AND LEFT
A silver sash pin (above) depicts the wildcat crest of the Sutherland Clan, against a background of Sutherland tartan. The same wildcat crest is also shown left as part of a book-plate bearing the Sutherland coat-of-arms. The family motto "sans peur" (French for "without fear"), is a pun on the word "purr".

Scotland, where the wildcat still survives in places, Clan Chattan, whose chief was known as the Great Wildcat (*Mohr au Chat*), used a cat symbol emblazoned with the motto "Touch not the cat but with a glove." Clan Mackintosh is one of several other Scottish clans to feature wildcats, in this case upon the helm of their armorial bearings.

Cats and *Luck*

....

Throughout history, the cat has been both venerated and reviled, so it is hardly surprising that it has been associated with both good and bad luck. Black cats were once seen as the devil's agents and long thought of as bringers of evil, although today they are commonly regarded as a good luck charm, especially in Britain. Charles I, King of Scotland and England from 1625 to 1649, is said to have had a lucky black cat, which died the day before the king's arrest

Théophile Steinlen's poster for a cabaret called the Chat Noir, *depicting an equivocal black cat which could be interpreted either as a symbol of evil or a bringer of good luck.*

leading to trial and execution by the Parliamentary forces who opposed him in the English Civil War. In the USA it is bad luck for a black cat to cross your path, whereas in Britain it is lucky – but originally this was only because once the cat had gone it meant bad luck had passed you by. In Brittany, France, it was believed that all black cats had at least one white hair – if you could pluck it out, it would bring you wealth as well as luck in love. The white cat is the tradition-al bringer of luck in the USA, except at night, when it, too, is deemed unlucky.

In Europe, there was a strong belief in the *matagot*, a benificent cat that would bring prosperity to those who cared for it. Puss-in-Boots, the cat in Charles Perrault's fairytale, is a prime example of a *matagot*. In the story, a clever cat is the only possession left by a father to his poor son, who can see no use for the cat except to eat him and make a muff from his skin. However, Puss persuades the young man to pro-vide him with boots and a satchel, and through his cunning ways, the cat wins his master an ogre's estate and the king's daughter in mar-riage. As for Puss, he too becomes a great lord and instead of having to hunt for his living, only does so for his own pleasure. Puss appears in many earlier forms of the story, including a sixteenth-century Italian version by Giovanni Francesco, and features in the folk traditions of many countries, although sometimes the protagonist is not a cat – in Indian myth he becomes a jackal, and in the Swahili version he is a gazelle-in-boots.

In the USA especially, white cats are symbols of good luck. Tinkie, *painted here by Derold Page, looks confident of bringing good fortune to his keepers.*

Scandinavian countries had their own protective cat, the Butter Cat. An animal with a particular liking for a bowl of cream, and a bringer of good fortune, in Finland the Butter Cat was also given the specific name of "Para", and farther north in Lapland it was known as "Smieragatto".

In the Far East, Buddhists regarded all cats as lucky and the Chinese believed in their powers of protection as keen feline senses would warn of the approach of demons in the darkness. Cats certainly were effective at getting rid of rats, and, when real cats were not available, pottery figures of felines, with candles burning inside them to ward off both vermin and evil spirits, were used instead.

To the Japanese the most lucky of cats is the tortoiseshell-and-white, the *mi-ke neko*. Japanese sailors, especially, were keen to have one aboard to ensure good winds and fair weather. Japan also has its form of *matagot* – in this case a tradition linked with a particular cat which lived at Gotoko-ji, a temple a few miles from the capital Edo (modern Tokyo), now swallowed up in the city's sprawl. Gotoko-ji was a poor Buddhist temple where few people made offerings until, one day, when a party of samurai were making their way back to their lord's castle, they saw a cat beside the road holding up a paw and apparently beckoning to them. The warriors were intrigued. Thinking that this may be an omen of some significance, they followed the cat up to the temple. There, the guardian monk served them tea in the traditional manner, discoursed with them on religious matters and encouraged them to rest. While the samurai were in the temple, there was a violent storm and the warriors were very thankful that the cat had saved them from it. When he heard their story, their lord was impressed enough to become patron of the temple and eventually his family shrine was established there. Gotoko-ji has also

Maneki-neko figures, on sale in Tokyo as talismans for good luck, commemorate the famous cat which brought good fortune to its temple, the Gotoko-ji.

become a shrine to which people come to pray for their cats. Thus the beckoning cat, the *maneki-neko*, brought good fortune to the temple and since has become a potent good luck symbol. Carved or modelled in pottery, it is kept in homes to bring people luck and displayed in shops and eating places to welcome customers and bestow its blessings. With today's interaction of world cultures you can also find the *maneki-neko* in many Western homes.

In London, at the Savoy Hotel, you will sometimes see another cat figure whose role, if not to bring good luck, is at least to ensure that no bad luck befalls customers in the famous restaurant. He is a large wooden cat called Kaspar, who serves as an additional guest should the party at any table number an unlucky thirteen. When his services are called upon, a complete table setting is placed before him, a napkin is set around his neck and each course is served to him throughout the meal. At three feet (90cm) in height, you are unlikely to miss him if he is sitting at your table.

Theatre folk are often highly superstitious, and certainly the presence of a cat backstage is thought to bring good luck. As in the tradition where, in order to wish an actor good luck in a performance, you bid him "break a leg", it is believed that if a cat fouls backstage, the performance will go well. Cats on stage, however, are a different matter and are often thought unlucky.

Many people, who would not usually regard themselves as superstitious, carry a charm or talisman of some kind or have a mascot. Sports teams and military units often have mascots, and during World War II, some airmen in Britain's Royal Air Force were known to take cats with them on operational missions. One cat that notched up more flights than most was Windy, the pet of Wing-Commander Guy Gibson, leader of the famous dambuster raid which ensured that Hitler could not develop an atomic bomb before the Allies.

"Kiss the black cat
And that'll make you fat:
Kiss the white one
And that'll make you lean."

by Sir John Denham (17th century)

Cat People

The witches of European tradition were thought to be able to turn themselves into felines but they were not the only ones capable of cat metamorphosis. In myth and legend, if not in fact, tales abound of cats who could change into humans, as well as people who were turned into cats by others, and some who, under certain conditions, became werecats quite unintentionally, in much the same way that others were transformed into werewolves.

One of Aesop's fables tells of a young man who became so enamoured of a cat, and she as doting on him, that he beseeched Venus, the Roman goddess of

Half-man and Half-cat is emblazoned across this German wood-carving (early 16th century). Although witches usually undergo metamorphosis, legend describes the transformation of other humans too.

love, for her help. Venus turned the cat into a beautiful young woman and the two were married. However, on their wedding night, the bride heard a mouse and instinctively leapt out of bed to chase it, and the goddess, offended by this ingratitude, immediately changed the bride back into a cat. The moral of the tale is that we can change our appearance, but we can never alter who we are inside.

Most cat-to-human transformations are more sinister. A Japanese story tells of the Vampire Cat of Nabeshima who kills the concubine of the Prince of Hizen, then buries her body and takes her form. Eventually the blood-sucker is hunted down and killed. Hollywood added to the mythology of metamorphosis with Jacques Tourneur's film *Cat People*, in which a beautiful Yugoslav girl believes she can turn into a panther and attacks several friends before she is discovered dead.

A Brazilian samba school parades as jaguars and ocelots in Rio's carnival. They wear their spots for fun but several movies feature werecats who turn out to be murderous panthers. Tabby Clovis in Stephen King's Sleepwalkers *sets the record straight for cats by leading a group of them against such evil shape-shifters.*

Psychic Cats

Have you ever witnessed your cat react to something that you could neither hear nor see? Many cat owners share this experience, and it is not explained by better hearing, vision or sense of smell – instead it seems to be a mysterious "sixth sense". Investigators of psychic phenomena claim that changes in air pressure and temperature accompany such ghostly manifestations, and that cats are highly attuned to them. And if cats can see ghosts, does it follow that ghost cats exist? Or is it only our imagination in overdrive when we think we see or feel the presence of deceased cats?

In some beliefs, such as Buddhism and Pythagorean theory, souls transmigrate from one lifeform to another, and in some Eastern countries the spirits of dead people are thought to enter cats. When Britain governed India in the nineteenth century, sentries at Government House, near Poona, would salute any cat that entered through the front door after sunset. Sir Robert Grant, Governor of Bombay, had died there in 1838 and it was believed that his spirit had entered one of the household cats. As no one was sure which cat was now the Governor, all were saluted.

It is very difficult to establish firm evidence of paranormal activity, but it is possible to quantify changes in a

Psyche, the white longhair in this painting by Francis Sartorius (1734–1804), certainly looks as if she might have seen a ghost. Cats often react to sights and sounds that are imperceptible to humans.

cat's behaviour that seem to indicate that the creature knows something that we don't. Mysouff, a cat belonging to French writer Alexandre Dumas, is a good example. He always accompanied Dumas when the owner left the house each morning, and once they parted at a certain spot, Mysouff would turn back. Later each day, at the same time, Mysouff was let out, and he would return to the same spot to meet Dumas on his way home. However, amazingly Mysouff seemed to know when Dumas was going to be late coming back: the door would be opened for Mysouff at the usual time, but the cat would stay curled up on a cushion, refusing to budge, somehow knowing that to leave would be futile.

Witches' Cats

This porcelain Inca figure shows a wildcat with the body of a serpent. It is thought to date from the Early Intermediate Period (c.100BCE– c.500CE). Cats were both magical and sacred to the Inca, who believed that their country was a puma straddling the Andes.

Cats have symbolized fertility from ancient times. To many members of the medieval Christian Church they were strongly linked with the mother goddess and pagan cults. It is hardly surprising, then, that they became associated with witchcraft and were condemned as evil representatives of the Devil. They were often persecuted alongside their keepers, usually old ladies, who were conveniently branded witches.

Sathan was an elderly, white spotted cat, belonging to a certain Elizabeth Francis, who, in 1566, was tried for witchcraft at Chelmsford in eastern England. It was said that Sathan practised all kinds of black magic in return for a few drops of his mistress's blood. According to some sources, Elizabeth Francis once gave the cat to her friend, Agnes Waterhouse, for whom Sathan drowned a cow and killed a goose belonging to the woman's neighbours. Elizabeth was one of many who were tried as witches in late-sixteenth- and seventeenth-century Britain, and accused of having animals as "familiars", or demon helpers. The familiars could be any small animals – dogs, goats, rabbits, newts, toads, but they were frequently cats – and witches were believed to suckle them through a third nipple located somewhere on their bodies.

At St Osyth, England, in 1582, eight-year-old Thomas Rabbet gave evidence that his mother had four familiars, including a lamb, a toad, their black cat Tibb, and a gray cat called Titty. Two women accused with her were said to have four "imps" in the form of cats. A Lancashire witch said her familiar, also named Tibb, could appear in the guise of a cat, a boy, a dog or a hare.

In 1618, Joan Flower participated in a plot to kill the Earl of Rutland's children using magic. She told how she stroked her cat, Rutterkin, with a glove stolen from one child while uttering words of magic, but when she tried the same spell with a handkerchief belonging to the other child, "Rutterkin whined and cried ... and had no power over the Lady Katherine to hurt her." In the same year, Ellen Green sent her cat, Puss, to bewitch and kill a baker, while Frances Moore confessed that her cat, Tissy, would lick blood from her finger before she sent him to put a death spell on someone.

Early settlers in the USA brought with them their belief in witchcraft. One of the most famous of all witch trials took place at Salem in Massachusetts in 1692. In total 150 people there were accused. Of these, 50 were aquitted, 13 were hanged, one was pressed to death, and one died naturally in prison. The lives of the rest were saved by a change in the rules of evidence. A man called Robert Downer, giving evidence against one Susanna Martin, said that the night after she told him that a she-devil would "shortly fetch him away", a demon in the shape of a cat came in through his window while he was in bed, and grabbed him by the throat. He believed it would have killed him if he had not invoked the names of the Holy Trinity. It then jumped off him and flew out of the window – perhaps Downer believed that it was the witch herself in cat form.

This witch, from Wright's History of Caricature and the Grotesque in Literature *(1865), is riding on a devil-faced goat, brandishing a demon cat. It was copied from a carving in a French cathedral.*

Dancing cat demons, with double tails, attend the Witch of Okabe, in a 19th-century Japanese woodcut print by Yoshifuji.

98

*The witch in
The Love Potion,
by Evelyn de Morgan
(1850–1919), is
accompanied here
by her "familiar",
a black cat. Familiars
were thought to be
servants of the Devil,
which would carry
out errands and spells
on behalf of witches.*

Cat "familiars" are less often linked with witches in Continental Europe than in Britain or the USA, although the last European witch to be executed, in 1749, was a Bavarian nun who confessed to having three cats in her room that were really devils in disguise. A more widespread belief was that a witch or warlock (a male witch) could take the shape of a cat. One typical story relates how a Scottish witch, as part of her testimony, gave the court details of the spells she used to turn herself into a cat and back again. Often the supposed witches in such accounts were identifed because they bore an injury similar to that which had been inflicted earlier on a supposedly demonic cat.

A Scandinavian tale concerns a mill that on the same date for two consecutive years mysteriously burned to the ground. In the third year, suspecting witchcraft, the miller decided to keep watch. He

In this colour lithograph, Hans Thoma offers a traditional portrayal of The Witch *as a hag, stirring her cauldron while she reads a spell and her cat watches.*

drew a magic circle for protection and settled down in its centre. Eventually a group of cats appeared, but they were not behaving like cats at all. They lit a fire, then set upon it a pot of pitch. When they swung the pot to spill the pitch and spread the flame, the miller could not stop himself from crying out, and gave himself away. The leading cat-witch then reached out and grabbed his arm, nearly pulling him out of the protective circle, but with his free hand he managed to draw a knife and slash off her paw. The witches then disappeared and he extinguished the fire and saved his mill. However, when he woke the next morning he discovered that his own wife had had her hand cut off at the wrist.

A similar, American story tells of a man who took on a bet to stay up all night in the Ozark Mountains, Missouri, said to be frequented by witches. He knocked back whisky to fortify his courage and he was already drunk and sleepy when, at midnight, a huge cat appeared. It attacked him and he remembered to fire his pistol only just in time. He then heard a woman scream and thought that he saw a bleeding human foot before the figure disappeared into the darkness. The next day a woman was discovered claiming to have accidentally shot herself in the foot. She died soon after from loss of blood.

Cats in Heaven and
Hell

....

Eastern tradition often links cats with heaven, for example, as the vessels that bear dead souls. In Islam, the cat itself is promised a place in heaven.

In Christian symbolism, and in paintings of the Virgin Mary, especially of the Annunciation and depictions of the Madonna and Child, a cat may seem to have a natural role in a domestic setting as the household mouser or the pet of the infant Jesus. But more often it is a symbol of the Devil. The appearance of the Annunciation angel makes the painted cat seem to flee in terror; the cat in the

Madonna and Child is usually there to represent the lurking danger in Christ's life – an omnipresent reminder of the suffering to come. In paintings of the Last Supper, a cat is sometimes shown placed near to the traitor Judas as a symbol of the Devil, and it is often opposed by a dog, a symbol of faithfulness.

Black cats, especially, were linked with the Devil. In the fourteenth century, when the Knights Templar were accused of worshipping him in the form of a big black cat called Baphomet, torture produced the expected confessions and the Order was suppressed.

In this cartoon by Thomas Rowlandson (1756–1827), Humbugging or Raising the Devil, *a stage conjuror calls up the Devil, while a cat is shown in attendance as an evil minion.*

"For he is an instrument for the children to
learn benevolence upon.
For every house is incomplete without him and
a blessing is lacking in the spirit."

from JUBILATE AGNO
by Christopher Smart (1854)

99 Cats' Log

....

The consecutive numbers here correspond to the gray numbers that enumerate the 99 cats in the text. Where several cats appear on one page, the page number is given only in the first instance.

1 PAGE 15
Sarah Snow, a green-eyed, long-haired white, would sit on Amis's lap as he wrote.

2 PAGE 15
Sachiko chased off all invaders no matter how big and tough they were.

3 PAGE 16
Gros Minou recovered after a long fall. A short fall often results in more injuries, as there is less time to right the body.

4
How could **Ricki** locate a survivor in the sea? Perhaps it was acute sight or hearing, or even the scent of human fear?

5 PAGE 18
Josie woke Mr and Mrs Miller by pushing her way beneath their bedsheets.

6 PAGE 19
Bomber probably learned that the sound of German airplanes was a threat by observing human reactions.

7 PAGE 20
McCavity was named after the criminal in Eliot's *Old Possum's Book of Practical Cats*.

8 PAGE 21
Beau Chat had some distinctive scars that identified him.

9
Sugar had a hip deformity that proved who he was.

10 PAGE 22
Pulcinella may have been named after a mischievous character in a traditional Italian folktale.

11 PAGE 23
Cody would jump down as soon as the music stopped.

12 PAGE 25
Tom was not seen at all by the Caras household after Pamela left home.

13 PAGE 31
Sizi lived at Schweizer's clinic in Gabon.

14 PAGE 33
Sampson had to learn to come home earlier or his keepers locked him out.

15 PAGE 34
Sumac repeated her escape several times, after which the window was kept shut.

16 PAGE 35
Boo Boo saved Luther Cruswell by waking him after he had slept through the smoke alarm.

17
Duke stayed in the burning house until all the family had left, sacrificing his own life.

18
Mouse wounded the intruder, which helped the police to identify the culprit.

19
If **Mi-Kitten** had not given the alarm, Walt probably would have died.

20
Willy had a keen sense of time in general and always got home promptly to be fed.

21 PAGE 38
Harvey was fortunate that the wash was not a big one and left some air space.

22
Surprisingly, **Susan** had a completely

normal ear at birth – the fold developed later on in her life.

23 PAGE 39
Kallibunker's pregnant granddaughter, Lamorna Cove, went to the USA in 1957 and established the breed there.

24
Kirlee was the only curly-coated kitten in his litter.

25
Prune's lack of fur meant that she was vulnerable to extreme temperatures.

26 and 27 PAGE 41
Inca and **Ariel**'s caching of objects may be linked to carrying prey back to the nest.

28 PAGE 43
Fa-Shen fell four stories on one occasion, cracking her upper palate in the process.

29 PAGE 51
Tarawood Antigone was four years old when she had her record litter.

30
Faith's bravery earned her the epitaph of "the bravest little cat in all the world".

31 PAGE 52
Himmy measured 33in (84cm) around his middle and was 38in (97cm) long excluding his tail.

32 PAGE 53
Charlie Chan's substantial inheritance included a house and a pet cemetery.

33 PAGE 54
Don Pierrot de Navarre used to listen to literary conversations and made sounds as if adding his opinion.

34 PAGE 56
The purpose of **Pudlenka** was to "replace a hundredfold" Capek's deceased cat.

35
Charles sometimes asked for a drawer to be pulled out so that he could sleep in it.

36 PAGE 57
The fictional **Saha** is so important to Alain that his wife Camille becomes jealous.

37
Chandler always read his detective stories to **Taki** before he began any rewrites.

38
Catarina inspired the spectral cat in Poe's tale *The Black Cat*.

39
Williamina was called William until it was discovered that she was pregnant.

40
The Master's Cat once stopped Dickens reading by trying to snuff out his candle.

41 PAGE 64
Minette sat on Mind's lap as he worked and sometimes Mind also had two kittens perched on his shoulders.

42
Tiger turned up at four in the morning, tired, dirty and ravenously hungry.

43 PAGE 65
Peter was a black-and-white cat who was a devoted companion for Wain's wife while she was ill.

44 PAGE 66
Hinse, the brindled cat, converted Scott to "liking a cat, an animal I detested".

45
Pepper refused to appear with any dogs other than Teddy. After the hound's death, he deserted the studio and disappeared.

46 PAGE 67
Timmie allowed the canary, Caruso, to sleep between his paws.

47 PAGE 71
Towser was succeeded by a tabby called Mr Toddy who was kidnapped after only a year's service.

48 PAGE 72
Gyb was a common 16th-century name for a cat. There was one in the play *Gammer Gurton's Needle*, performed in 1548.

49 PAGE 73

Mysouff was a black-and-white cat discovered in the cellar by Dumas' cook.

50

Madame Théophile had a habit of trying to steal food from Gautier's fork as he ate.

51 PAGE 74

Mr Moody's cat usually caught minnows and occasionally eels and pilchards.

52

Rybolov, like bears and jaguars, must have used the flipping technique to reach down from the icy surface.

53 PAGE 75

Selima was immortalized in poetry by Walpole's friend, the English lyric poet Thomas Gray (1716–1771).

54

Ariel would also retrieve a catnip mouse as often as Van Vechten threw it for her.

55 PAGE 80

mehitabel first appeared in 1916 in Don Marquis' Chicago newspaper column.

56 PAGE 83

Mandy loved playing with a table-tennis ball, especially with a human partner.

57 PAGE 85

Mike's obituary was written by the great Egyptologist Sir Ernest Wallis Budge.

58 PAGE 86

Smudge was modelled life-size, in 1986, by ceramic artist Margery Clinton, and later in a half-size version.

59

Tiddles collected considerable sums for animal charities in a saucer by his basket.

60

Beerbohm was named after Herbert Beerbohm Tree, the Victorian actor.

61 PAGE 87

Feedback also spends much of his time greeting visitors in the lobby.

62

The original **Arthur** died in 1976 at the ripe old age of nearly 17.

63

Morris had his own limousine and a Louis Vuitton litter tray.

64

Orangey was dubbed by one movie director "the world's meanest cat".

65

Mourka was no doubt rewarded for his bravery as the building where he delivered his messages also housed a kitchen.

66 PAGE 92

Dick Whittington's cat was added to the tale long after the events actually occurred,

and may have derived from the misinterpretation of the word "achat" in the original story, which meant to buy favours.

67 PAGE 93

Oscar spent the rest of his days ashore, relaxing in a sailor's home.

68 PAGE 94

Simon was the only cat among animals in the British Armed Services during World War II to win a Dickens Medal.

69

Charlie was killed on duty and was buried with full military honours.

70 PAGE 97

Bastet was sometimes known as the Little Cat; her lioness sisters Sekhmet and Tefnet were the Big Cats.

71 PAGE 98

Nabumen's cat perches on papyrus stems. This unlikely pose forms part of the case for arguing that the cat appears only symbolically as a vessel of souls to the afterlife.

72 PAGE 99

Lisa's breed, the Egyptian Mau, should never be called Mau cats as "mau" is actually the Egyptian word for cat.

73 PAGE 101

Siam completed her arduous journey to Washington in 1878 but sadly died a few months later.

74 and 75

Some breeders are seeking to return to the rounded forms of **Mia** and **Pho**, rather than the angular Siamese shapes of today.

76 PAGE 104

Slippers also had the distinction of being hexadactylic – his paws had six toes.

77 PAGE 105

Tom Kitten was named after the character in Beatrix Potter's stories.

78

Socks was the first First Cat to have his own website on the internet. He regularly makes appearances in political cartoons.

79 PAGE 106

Myobu No Omoto was once chased by a dog, a crime so heinous that the dog was exiled and its owner put in prison.

80

Louis XV, pretending to be his **white cat**, once crept up behind the Duc de Noailles, meowing grotesquely – the Duc fainted.

81

Nelson had his own special chairs at the dining table and in the Cabinet Room at 10 Downing Street.

82 PAGE 107

Wilberforce was Office Manager's cat during Heath's administration (1970–1974).

83

Humphrey was said to have disappeared after Tony Blair moved into Downing Street in 1997. He soon re-emerged for the press, but was retired shortly afterward.

84 PAGE 108

Muezza's name is a form of "muezzin", the name for the man who calls the faithful to prayer in Islamic practice.

85 PAGE 109

Soumise and Cardinal Richelieu's other cats were burned to death by soldiers, just like the witches' cats whose deaths their late master had ordered.

86

When one of the archbishop's chaplains was asked to feed **Desdemona**, the butler intervened remarking, "la Signora will prefer waiting for the roasts."

87 PAGE 114

Grippeminaud heads the Furrycats, a tribe that live by bribery and corruption.

88

Koko was inspired by Jackson's own Siamese who was killed when pushed out of a window by a demented woman.

89 and 90 PAGE 115

Francis and his associate **Bluebeard** unravel a complex plot behind a series of grisly murders in the cat community.

91

Zola's unnamed Angora was criticized for his lifestyle by his alley cat friend who piously declared that meat and soft pillows are never worth imprisonment.

92

No-name introduces his readers to his girlfriends – a white cat who lives opposite and a beautiful tortoiseshell.

93 PAGE 121

Kaspar was carved by sculptor Basil Ionides in the 1920s.

94 PAGE 125

The Vampire Cat casts a spell to make the Prince's sentries sleep, but is outwitted by a faithful retainer who stays awake.

95 PAGE 128

Sathan was allegedly able to turn himself into a toad as one of his tricks.

96 and 97

Tibb and **Titty** are such innocent names to be given to devils, but perhaps this only served to emphasize their apparent evil.

98 PAGE 129

Tissy takes blood from her mistress's finger. Many witches were said to suckle cats.

99 PAGE 133

Baphomet was thought to be the name of a demon in the Middle Ages.

Index

....

Bibliography

Altman, Roberta. *The Quintessential Cat*, Macmillan, New York, 1994, and Blandford Press, London, 1995

Boylan, Clare. *The Literary Companion to Cats*, Sinclair-Stevenson, London, 1995

Davies, Marion. *The Magical Lore of Cats*, Capall Bann, Berkshire, England, 1995

Exley, Helen. *Glorious Cats*, Exley Publications Ltd, Watford, England, and Exley Gift Books, New York, both 1995

Greene, David. *Incredible Cats*, Methuen, London, 1995

Loxton, Howard. *The Noble Cat*, Portland House, New York, 1990

Morris, Desmond. *Catworld*, Ebury Press, London, 1996, and Penguin Books, New York, 1997

Nown, Graham and Nown, Silvana. *A Clowder of Cats*, Futura, New York, 1989

Repplier, Agnes. *The Fireside Sphinx*, Gay and Bird, London, 1901

Saunders, Nicholas, J. *Animal Spirits*, Macmillan, London, and Time-Life Books, Virginia, both 1995

Tabor, Roger. *The Wild Life of the Domestic Cat*, Arrow Books, London, 1993

Walker, Ann. *Cats' Company*, Capall Bann, Berkshire, England, 1995

Wheen, Francis. *The Chatto Book of Cats*, Chatto & Windus Ltd, London, 1993

Picture Credits

Library, London; **37** Thomas Amman Fine Art and The Lefevre Gallery, London/A.K.G. London © ADAGP, Paris and DACS, London 1998; **38** Iona Antiques, London/Bridgeman Art Library, London; **39** Private Collection/Bridgeman Art Library, London; **40** Bonhams, London/Bridgeman Art Library, London, © The Estate of Louis Wain; **42** Anne Wilson; **43t** O'Shea Gallery/Bridgeman Art Library, London; **43b** Private Collection/E.T. Archive, London, © The Estate of Louis Wain; **44** Magnum Photos, London/Martine Franck; **47** Bonhams, London/Bridgeman Art Library, London; **48t** Nationalmuseum, Stockholm/National Gallery, London; **48b** Private Collection/Bridgeman Art Library, London; **49** Museum für Kunstsammlung Nordrhein-Westfalen, Düsseldorf/A.K.G. London; **50** Private Collection/Bridgeman Art Library, London; **51** Gavin Graham Gallery, London/Bridgeman Art Library, London; **52l** Musée d'Orsay, Paris/A.K.G. London; **52r** Musée de Petit Palais, Geneva/A.K.G. London; **54** Private Collection/A.K.G. London; **55** Kunsthaus, Zurich/Giraudon Superstock, Paris; **57** Magnum Photos, London/George Rodger; **58** A.K.G. London/Paul Almasy; **60** A.K.G. London/Paul Almasy; **62** Phillips Fine Art Auctioneers, London/Bridgeman Art Library, London, © ADAGP, Paris and DACS, London 1998; **63l** Magnum Photos, London/Roger Capa; **63r** Private Collection/Fortean Picture Library, Clwyd; **65** Roy Miles Gallery, London/Bridgeman Art Library, London; **66** Crane Gallery, London/Bridgeman Art Library, London, by Derold Page; **68** The British Museum, London/Michael Holford, Loughton; **69** Private Collection/Bridgeman Art Library, London, © The Estate of Eric Ravilious. All Rights Reserved, DACS 1998; **70** National Museum of Naples/A.K.G. London/Erich Lessing; **71** Musée d'Orsay, Paris/Bridgeman Art Library, London, © ADAGP, Paris and DACS, London 1998; **72** Picasso Museum, Paris/Giraudon Superstock, Paris, © Succession Picasso/DACS 1998; **73a** The British Library, London/Bridgeman Art Library, London; **73b** B.W. Robinson Collection/E.T. Archive, London; **74** Stern Art Dealers, London/Bridgeman Art Library, London; **75** Bonhams, London/Bridgeman Art Library, London; **76** Magnum Photos, London/Henri Cartier-Bresson; **79** Palacio de los Fronteira, Lisbon/E.T. Archive, London; **81** Private Collection/Bridgeman Art

Library, London, © Bridgeman Art Library, London; **83** Private Collection/Bridgeman Art Library, London, by Timothy Easton; **84** Gavin Graham Gallery, London/Bridgeman Art Library London; **85l** The British Library, London/E.T. Archive, London; **85r** Archiv für Kunst & Geschichte, Berlin/A.K.G. London; **86l** The British Museum London/Michael Holford, Loughton; **86r** The Advertising Archives, London; **87** Musée de la Publicité, Paris/A.K.G. London; **88–9** Magnum Photos, London/Larry Towell; **90–91** Magnum Photos, London/Morath Inge; **93** Annora Spence, London; **94** Viewpoint Projects, London/Howard Loxton; **96** E.T. Archive, London; **97** Louvre, Paris/Bridgeman Art Library, London; **98** British Museum/E.T. Archive, London; **99a** Fitzwilliam Museum, Cambridge/Bridgeman Art Library, London; **99b** The British Museum, London; **100** The British Museum, London; **101** Hutchison Picture Library, London/Jackum Brown; **102** National Gallery of Art, Washington D.C./Bridgeman Art Library, London; **103** Shelbourne Museum, Vermont/E.T. Archive, London; **105** Associated Press AP. London/Marcy Nighswander; **107** Boughton House, Northamptonshire/Bridgeman Art Library, London; **108** Trinity College, Dublin; **109** St Sulpice, Diest, Belgium/Fortean Picture Library, Clywd; **110–11** Magnum Photos, London/Martine Franck; **113** Belgrade National Museum/A.K.G. London; **114** Stapleton Collection, London/Bridgeman Art Library, London, © ADAGP, Paris and DACS, London 1998; **115** Copyright Frederick Warne and Co., London, © ADAGP, Paris and DACS, London, 1998 **116l** and **116r** Jamie Sutherland, London; **118** Musée de la Publicité, Paris/A.K.G. London; **119** Private Collection/Bridgeman Art Library, London, by Derold Page; **120** Viewpoint Project, London/ Howard Loxton; **121** Anne Wilson; **122–3** Magnum Photos London/Michael Nichols; **124** Private Collection/Fortean Picture Library, Clywdd; **125** South American Pictures/Tony Morrison, Woodbridge; **126** Fenton House, London/National Trust Photographic Library/Derrick E. Witty; **128** Archaelogical Museum, Lima/E.T. Archive, London; **128–9** Private Collection/Fortean Picture Library, Clywdd; **129** Private Collection/E.T. Archive, London; **130** De Morgan Foundation, London/Bridgeman Art Library, London; **131** Archiv für Kunst & Geschichte, Berlin/A.K.G. London; **133** Private Collection/Michael Holford, Loughton; **134** Magnum Photos, London/Henri Cartier-Bresson